# National PSI Exam Prep

Sherry Steele,
Contributing Editor

Fourth Edition

This publication is designed to provide accurate and authoritative information in regard to the subject matter covered. It is sold with the understanding that the publisher is not engaged in rendering legal, accounting, or other professional advice. If legal advice or other expert assistance is required, the services of a competent professional should be sought.

President: Dr. Andrew Temte
Chief Learning Officer: Dr. Tim Smaby
Executive Director, Real Estate Education: Melissa Kleeman-Moy
Development Editor: Kari Domeyer

NATIONAL PSI EXAM PREP FOURTH EDITION
©2014 Kaplan, Inc.
Published by DF Institute, Inc., d/b/a Dearborn Real Estate Education
332 Front St. S., Suite 501
La Crosse, WI 54601

Printed in the United States of America

ISBN: 978-1-4754-2322-8 / 1-4754-2322-5
PPN: 2135-9205

# Contents

Preparing for the Exam Prep Course   v

**UNIT 1**
General Principles of Agency   1

**UNIT 2**
Contracts   9

**UNIT 3**
Practice of Real Estate   15

**UNIT 4**
Financing   23

**UNIT 5**
Valuation and Market Analysis   33

**UNIT 6**
Property Ownership   39

**UNIT 7**
Land-Use Controls and Regulations   47

**UNIT 8**
Specialty Areas   53

**UNIT 9**
Mandated Disclosures   55

**UNIT 10**
Transfer of Title    59

**UNIT 11**
Real Estate Math Review    67

**UNIT 12**
National Portion True/False Questions    91

**APPENDIX**
Self-Score Answer Sheets    149

# Preparing for the Exam Prep Course

Welcome to Exam Prep! Take these steps to get the most out of the course:

1. Read this section ("Preparing for the Exam Prep Course") in its entirety.
2. Complete the true/false questions before you attend the course or view the online lectures.
3. Bring this workbook to class (or use with the online lectures).

**It is very important to read this section before proceeding with the course.**

Exam Prep is the most accurate predictor of whether you are ready for the actual licensing exam. The course consists of two full-length practice exams and two content review sessions. Each practice exam consists of the same two portions you will face on the actual licensing exam (a national portion and a state portion).

## ■ WHAT SHOULD YOU DO TO PREPARE FOR THE EXAM PREP COURSE?

Follow these steps to prepare for this Exam Prep course and to ensure a successful study program:

1. If you are taking Kaplan's real estate licensing program in its entirety, you should complete and pass all coursework and exams in the program before starting this Exam Prep course.
2. Complete all of the true/false questions in this book.
   - ■ Start with your weakest topic.
   - ■ Conceal the answers on the right-hand side and try to determine whether each statement is true or false.
     - — If the statement is false, see if you can change it to make it true. For example:

   | 1. Colorado is a country in South America. | F Colorado is a state in the United States in North America. |

   - — Before revealing the answer, you should have answered "false" and changed the statement to "North America."
   - — If you know a statement is false but do not know how to make it true, mark the question as missed.
   - ■ When you are done with all the questions in a section, evaluate how you did on that topic. If you missed several questions, use the Exam Prep Strength and Weakness Indicator Chart on the following pages to find out where to review that topic.
   - ■ Once you have completed all the true/false questions, retake the ones you got wrong. If you miss them again, mark them. Continue retaking

the questions you got wrong until you don't miss anymore questions and completely understand all the concepts.

— The key is to always study what you do NOT know until you learn it.

3. Take the pre-test. Classroom students will take it in class; OnDemand and Home Study students will take it online.

■ Use a self-score answer sheet from the appendix. You will need this sheet to keep track of your results because each pre-test question will be reviewed during class. Bring this sheet with you to class or have it available while you watch the online lectures.

■ Use your results to complete the Exam Prep Strength and Weakness Indicator Chart to identify your strong and weak areas.

■ To improve on your weak areas, redo the true/false questions for those topics. For the true/false questions you answered correctly, make sure you got them correct for the right reason (not just a lucky guess). For the questions you missed, use your course materials to review the concept being tested. Keep taking these questions until you are confident that you understand the underlying concepts.

4. Attend the Exam Prep lectures (or view them online). BRING YOUR PRE-TEST ANSWER SHEET WITH YOU.

5. Take the post-test. Use a self-score answer sheet from the appendix. This will allow you to identify how you performed in each question category.

■ Use your results to complete the Exam Prep Strength and Weakness Indicator Chart just as you did with the pre-test.

■ To improve on your weak areas, use the page references in the chart to review the relevant content. If you are taking the full Kaplan licensing program, you can also use your other course materials for review. Start by reviewing your weakest areas first.

■ Again, be sure to redo the true/false questions for the topics you need to brush up on. Keep taking these questions until you are confident that you understand the underlying concepts.

Register for your licensing exam with PSI at www.psiexams.com.

# ■ EXAM PREP STRENGTH AND WEAKNESS INDICATOR CHART

To use this chart, enter the number you answered correctly in each topic area. For the topics you need to work on, use the page references to go back and review the content in the book.

**SP = Salesperson; BK = Broker**

| Questions Answered Correctly | Topic Area | Exam Prep T/F Items | Exam Prep Outline | *Modern Real Estate Practice Workbook* Sections |
|---|---|---|---|---|
| Pre-Test _____ <br> Post-Test _____ | Valuation & Market Analysis (SP 8 questions; BK 6 questions) | pp. 119–124 | pp. 33–37 | Unit 6 – entire unit |
| Pre-Test _____ <br> Post-Test _____ | Financing (SP 6 questions; BK 7 questions) | pp. 108–116 | pp. 23–31 | Unit 7 – entire unit <br> Unit 8 – Loan Programs |
| Pre-Test _____ <br> Post-Test _____ | Contracts (SP 11 questions; BK 12 questions) | pp. 98–103 | pp. 9–14 | Unit 5 – entire unit |
| Pre-Test _____ <br> Post-Test _____ | Math—Valuation and Financing (SP 6 questions; BK 4 questions) | pp. 117–118; 125–126 | pp. 67–89 | See the Real Estate Math Review in Unit 11 of this book. |
| Pre-Test _____ <br> Post-Test _____ | Property Ownership (SP 7 questions; BK 6 questions) | pp. 127–134 | pp. 39–46 | Unit 1 – Real Estate/Real Property <br> Unit 2 – entire unit <br> Unit 3 – Forms of Ownership |
| Pre-Test _____ <br> Post-Test _____ | Transfer of Title (SP 5 questions; BK 5 questions) | pp. 142–148 | pp. 59–66 | Unit 3 – Deeds, Conveyance After Death, and Adverse Possession <br> Unit 4 – entire unit <br> Unit 8 – Income Taxation |
| Pre-Test _____ <br> Post-Test _____ | Land-Use Controls and Regulations (SP 5 questions; BK 5 questions) | pp. 135–138 | pp. 47–52 | Unit 1 – Government Land-Use Controls <br> Unit 2 – Governmental Rights in Land and Encumbrances |
| Pre-Test _____ <br> Post-Test _____ | General Principles of Agency (SP 10 questions; BK 11 questions) | pp. 92–97 | pp. 1–7 | Unit 9 – Agency |
| Pre-Test _____ <br> Post-Test _____ | Mandated Disclosures (SP 8 questions; BK 9 questions) | pp. 140–141 | pp. 55–57 | Unit 3 – Property Transfer Disclosures |
| Pre-Test _____ <br> Post-Test _____ | Practice of Real Estate (SP 12 questions; BK 12 questions) | pp. 104–107 | pp. 15–21 | Unit 8 – Truth in Lending Act, Fair Housing Laws, and ECOA |
| Pre-Test _____ <br> Post-Test _____ | Specialty Areas (SP 2 questions; BK 3 questions) | pp. 139 | pp. 53–54 | Unit 5 – Types of Leases |
| **Total Pre-Test** _____ <br> **Total Post-Test** _____ | | | | |

*If you answered at least 64 questions (out of 80) correct, you achieved a score of at least 80%.

# ■ WHAT SHOULD YOU DO IF YOU SCORE 80% OR HIGHER ON THE PRE-TEST?

**If you score 80% or higher on the Pre-Test.** You're doing well, but you may still need to focus on a few areas that you haven't quite mastered. You should do the following:

- ■ Use the Exam Prep Strength and Weakness Indicator Chart to identify the areas you still need to review.
- ■ Attend the Exam Prep lectures or view them online, paying special attention to your weak areas.
- ■ Take the Exam Prep Post-Test at the end of the course.

# ■ WHAT SHOULD YOU DO IF YOU SCORE LESS THAN 80% ON THE PRE-TEST?

**If you score 75 to 79% on the Pre-Test.** You're doing well, but you may need to focus on a few areas that you haven't quite mastered. You should do the following:

- Use the Exam Prep Strength and Weakness Indicator Chart to identify the areas you most need to review.
- Attend the Exam Prep lectures or view them online, paying special attention to your weak areas.
- Take the Post-Test at the end of the course if you are ready; if not, wait and take it when you feel prepared.
- If you have already scheduled your exam, evaluate whether you will have enough time to study after the Exam Prep course or if you should reschedule the exam.

**If you score less than 75% on the Pre-Test.** Students who score below 75% on the Pre-Test generally struggle to pass the actual licensing exam. But don't panic; you can pass it with more study.

- Consider waiting to complete Exam Prep. Often, spending additional time studying and completing or reviewing all the true/false questions will allow you to pass the Post-Test. If you decide that you want to wait, give yourself enough time to study and prepare (typically no more than 3 to 4 weeks). If you have already set a test date, remember you might need to cancel or reschedule it.
- Consult your Exam Prep Strength and Weakness Indicator Chart. This chart will help you identify the content areas in which you need to improve. Start your review with your weakest area first.
- Review real estate terms. Familiarity with real estate terms is crucial. If you're taking Kaplan's complete licensing program, review the key terms in your study materials. If you do not know a term, make a flashcard for yourself. Once you have completed the process, you will have a stack of flashcards to review. If you are not enrolled in Kaplan's entire licensing program, consider purchasing a good real estate dictionary. We have the best books in the industry available for sale on our website and at some of our school locations.
- Study the true/false questions in your Exam Prep book. You've probably reviewed these before, but try answering them again. If you've followed the preceding steps, the concepts tested in the true/false questions will be more familiar. Be sure to conceal the answers as you study the questions. For every false statement, try to change the information to make it a true statement. This will further ensure that you understand the concept being tested.

## ■ WHAT SHOULD YOU DO IF YOU SCORE LESS THAN 80% ON THE POST-TEST?

**If you score less than 80% on either portion of the Post-Test.**

■ The Post-Test is an accurate predictor of whether you're prepared to pass the actual licensing exam. Scores lower than 80% generally indicate you are not yet ready for the actual exam.

■ You need to review the material. If you're enrolled in Kaplan's complete licensing program, reread the relevant units in your materials, attend (or view online) selected class sessions, and work through the review exams until you're ready to try the Post-Test again. Review all the sections and areas you missed using the Exam Prep Strength and Weakness Indicator Chart. Review the true/false questions for those areas.

■ When you feel ready, retake the exam.

## ■ WE ARE HERE TO HELP

The faculty and staff at Kaplan Professional Schools are committed to your success on the licensing exam. Please contact us at any time throughout your studies to let us know how you are doing or how we may be of service.

**UNIT**

# General Principles of Agency

**(Test questions: Salesperson 10; Broker 11)**

## I. PARTIES TO AN AGENCY RELATIONSHIP

### A. Principal

1. A principal is one who employs another to act on her behalf.

2. **Agent owes fiduciary duties to the principal who <u>employs</u> him. <u>This may or may not be who pays the agent</u>.**

### B. Agent/fiduciary

1. An agent/fiduciary is a person who is employed to represent a principal.

2. A salesperson signing a listing will <u>NOT have the agency</u> relationship with the principal; it is between the firm and the principal.

### C. Subagent

1. Common-law definition is the person who is employed to represent an agent representing a principal.

### D. Third party—customer

1. A third party is a party to a transaction who is not a party to the particular agency agreement.

2. Agent owes honesty and fair dealing.

3. **At first contact with customers, agents must disclose that customers should not give confidential information to them.**

   a) Agents' fiduciary duties would require them to share that information with their principal.

## II. COMMON LAWS OF AGENCY

### A. Key points

1. Specify, through cases and ruling, each agent's **fiduciary** responsibilities of Obedience, Loyalty, Disclosure, Confidentiality, Accounting, and Reasonable care and skill (**OLD CAR**).

2. **The agent always owes fiduciary duties (obligations) to the principal who employed her.**

3. **The agent must keep confidential the price, terms, and motivation (PTM) of the principal.**

4. Accounting includes accounting for all money and <u>personal property</u> given to the broker.

5. **Note: Most states define agency relationship by statute; may see <u>common laws of agency</u> on national portion of exam.**

## B. Types of agency—created by a <u>fiduciary agreement</u>.

1. **Special agency** is created when a brokerage firm/agent is authorized to perform a particular act without the ability to bind the principal.

   a)  Seller contracts with a brokerage firm using a listing contract.

   b)  Buyer contracts with a brokerage firm using a buyer brokerage contract.

2. **General agency** is created when a brokerage firm/agent is authorized to perform a series of acts associated with the continued operation of a particular business (limited power to bind principal).

   a)  Salesperson is licensed to a broker.

   b)  **Property manager is employed by a property owner.**

3. **Universal agency** is created when a brokerage firm/agent is authorized to perform in place of the principal (total power to bind principal). A form called a power of attorney is used, which appoints the attorney-in-fact.

## C. Creation of agency

1. <u>Express agency</u> is created through an oral or <u>written listing or buyer representation agreement</u>.

2. **Implied agency** is created through the actions of the parties and should not be used for listing as it is not in writing.

3. Real estate contracts should be expressed.

## D. Liability for another's acts

1. Each employing broker is responsible for all professional acts and conduct performed by the broker or by a salesperson/associate broker working under him or her.

2. Brokers or salespersons may **not** misrepresent property or conceal material facts.

   a)  **If a broker or salesperson promised something such as, "I know the new light rail will run here," when in fact it doesn't, the broker would be guilty of material misrepresentation.**

## E. Disclosure of representation

1. Disclose representation, either orally or in writing, **prior to showing or receiving any <u>confidential information</u>.**

2. If representation changes, a new disclosure is required **at once**.

3. Must disclose if representing a relative or if licensee is the principal.

4. When representing both the buyer and the seller (dual agency), **the agent must get consent of both parties in writing.** Disclosure must state the source of any expected compensation to the broker. (Note: Dual agency is illegal in some states, but may appear on the national portion.)

## III.   PROPERTY MANAGEMENT

### A.   Property management—creates agency and representation agreement

1. Agreement is signed by the employing broker who then will be a <u>general agent</u> **of the landlord**

2. May not be signed by salesperson or broker associate without permission of the employing/managing broker

### B.   Property manager's obligations

1. Generates income and maintains the physical condition

2. **Markets space to attract tenants**

   a)   **Most important is <u>careful selection of the highest-qualified tenants</u>**

   b)   **Manager renting industrial property would be concerned about environmental issues**

3. Collects rents and security deposits

4. Develops annual budget and prepares financial reports

5. Negotiates leases, including investigating applicants' qualifications

6. **Does not spend the profits**

## IV.   THE LISTING AGREEMENT—CONTRACT IS OWNED BY THE BROKERAGE FIRM

### A.   Types of listings—broker may refuse to take any listing

1. Exclusive-right-to-sell listing

   a)   Brokerage firm paid **even if the seller** or someone else finds the buyer

   b)   Gives **maximum** broker protection by eliminating procuring cause disagreements

2. Exclusive–agency listing

   a)   Owner retains right to sell himself without paying a commission.

b)  If anyone other than the owner obtains the buyer, the brokerage firm gets paid.

c)  **Agent would put into MLS but would be less motivated due to competition from the seller.**

3.  Open/nonexclusive listing

a)  Owner may list with more than one brokerage or may just offer to pay anyone who brings an offer.

b)  Listing brokerage is paid only if the brokerage obtains buyer and **is the procuring cause** of the sale.

c)  May be terminated at any time prior to performance.

## B.  Essential elements of a listing

1.  **Express agreement**—in writing and signed

2.  **Commissions are <u>negotiable in all cases</u>.**

3.  Price and terms

4.  **Specific termination date**

## C.  How a listing terminates

1.  Performance by both parties (closing the sale)

a)  Even if the listing expires while the property is under contract, the listing broker agrees to close the transaction in order to receive a commission.

2.  Expiration on the termination date listed in the contract

3.  Mutual rescission

4.  Death or incapacity of either employing broker or seller **(Note: The death of salesperson/broker associate does not terminate a listing.)**

5.  **Destruction of premises (e.g., the house burns down)**

6.  Bankruptcy of either broker or seller

7.  Breach or failure to uphold the agreement by either the broker or seller

### D. Protection clause/extension clause/holdover clause/safety clause

1. This clause provides for a broker to collect a commission for a certain length of time after the termination of the listing, if a buyer the broker procured during the listing purchases the property.

    a) **Do not confuse with loan clauses such as alienation, acceleration, or co-insurance.**

2. Many states have laws that terminate this clause once seller signs new listing; otherwise, seller could potentially become liable for two commissions.

### E. Obligations of the listing broker

1. Present all written offers

2. Complete a written offer if buyer requests it

3. Only pay referral fees to other brokerage firms, never to the other firm's broker associates or salespeople

    a) No fees or commissions may be paid to unlicensed persons.

4. Put all agreements in writing, have them signed, and give all parties copies

5. Verify that all marketing is correct and truthful

    a) **Includes disclosure of material facts and property information such as property taxes, HOA dues, and so forth**

    b) Buyer has received seller's property disclosure **prior to making an offer.**

6. If a seller misrepresents a latent defect in the seller's property disclosure

    a) As long as the broker had performed a visual inspection and found no obvious defects, the broker would **not be held liable for the misrepresentation.**

### F. Obligations of all brokers and salespeople

1. Verify information and statements made by the buyer and seller, especially if they appear to be **untrue.**

2. **Complete a CMA to verify value, even if the broker or salesperson believes they know the current value.**

3. **Material facts must be <u>disclosed immediately to all parties</u>** (e.g., hail damage or roof issues).

4.  Complete a visual inspection of the property looking for material defects and request a seller's property disclosure.

    a)  **Recommend the buyer have an inspection** to check for latent defects and environmental issues.

    b)  Point out any "red flag" issues that may represent potential problems (sagging floors, water stains, etc.).

5.  Answer third-party questions with honesty and clarity.

## V.    BUYER AGENCY AGREEMENT

### A.  Buyer representation agreement

1.  Exclusive right to represent authorizes one broker to represent the buyer and requires the buyer to compensate the agent when purchasing property through any source.

2.  Termination is the same as listing agreements (death, bankruptcy, etc.). Buyer representation agreements must have a definite termination date.

3.  **An agent who showed property based on the potential commission, not because of the buyer's needs would be violating the fiduciary obligation of loyalty.**

4.  **A buyer who hired an agent using an Exclusive Agency contract would not pay a commission if the buyer found and bought a property on her own accord.**

## VI.    SHERMAN ANTITRUST ACT

### A.  Antitrust laws prohibit anticompetitive behavior such as price-fixing.

### B.  Price-fixing—competitors agree to charge the same rates.

1.  Price-fixing is illegal as it **inhibits competition.**

2.  The amount and method of compensation paid to the **listing broker** is negotiable.

    a)  Brokers must not be a party to discussions of commissions with those outside their office, such as one employing broker to another employing broker.

3.  Employing brokers may have commission side agreements with their salespeople or broker associates, but not with someone outside the firm.

4.  Brokers who overhear commission conversations of outside brokers should shout and get out of the room or area. (Say loudly, "I wouldn't talk about commissions outside of the office!" and then leave.)

# 2 UNIT

# Contracts

**(Test questions: Salesperson 11; Broker 12)**

## I.    THE STAGES OF A REAL ESTATE PURCHASE CONTRACT

| Stage: | 1. Listed | 2. Offer, acceptance, and communication of acceptance | 3. Under contract (with or without earnest money) | 4. Closing |
|---|---|---|---|---|
| Features: | On the market | Offeror—made last offer<br>Offeree—received last offer<br>Attachments—explain<br>Addendum/Addenda—attached to offers | Buyer (vendee) has equitable title (owner in equity)<br>Seller (vendor) retains legal title<br>Amendments modify contracts | Transfer of legal title to buyer<br><u>Deed:</u><br>Grantor = seller<br>Grantee = buyer |
| Key Point: | | Acceptance must be communicated to offeror to form binding contract. | Executory period | Executed |

## II.    CONTRACT BASICS

### A.  Definition of a contract

1.  A contract is a legally binding and enforceable agreement to do or not to do a specific thing.

2.  <u>Express</u>—can be oral or <u>**written**</u>.

3.  Implied—created by actions, not in writing.

4.  Statute of frauds requires contracts transferring real estate interests to be expressed written agreements.

### B.  Conditions of a contract

1.  A valid contract contains all essential elements, is binding on both parties, and is enforceable by the courts.

2.  **A voidable contract appears to be valid, but one party may disaffirm because the party is a minor or was subject to duress, fraud, or misrepresentation.**

3.  A void contract is not enforceable due to failure to contain all essential elements.

### C.  Parties to a contract

| Offer | One receiving offer = offeree (ee's receive) | One giving offer = offeror (or's give) | **Only document where the parties can change** |
|---|---|---|---|
| **Lease** | Tenant = lessee | Landlord = lessor | |
| **Option** | Buyer = optionee | Seller = optionor | |
| **Purchase agreement** | Buyer = vendee | Seller = vendor | |
| **Contract or contract for deed** | Buyer = vendee | Seller = vendor | |
| **Mortgage** | Lender = mortgagee | Buyer = mortgagor | |
| **Deed of trust** | Lender = beneficiary | Buyer = trustor | Third party = trustee |
| **Deed** | Buyer = grantee | Seller = grantor | |

## III.    PERFORMANCE AND DISCHARGE OF OBLIGATIONS

### A.    Unilateral versus bilateral

1.    Unilateral—promise is exchanged for performance.

    a)    Alice promises to perform ("I will sell you my house"), if Bill decides he wants Alice to perform ("I may buy your house; let me decide").

2.    Bilateral—promise is exchanged for a promise.

    a)    Alice and Bill make equal promises.

        (1)    Alice—"I promise to sell you my house and deliver a deed."

        (2)    Bill—"I promise to buy your house and pay you money."

### B.    Executed versus executory

1.    Executed—duties are completed by both parties; they are fully performed.

2.    **Executory—one or both parties need to complete part of the contract; duties yet to be performed.**

### C.    Assignment versus novation

1.    Assignment—transfers obligation but not liability (e.g., sublease).

2.    **Novation—a <u>new contract</u> replacing an old one; transfers obligation and liability.**

### D.    Legal impossibility/impossibility of performance

1.    A duty required by the contract can't be legally performed.

### E.    Death or incapacity

1.    Contract is terminated only if no one is left to perform.

### F.    Amendments

1.    Changes or modifications to a contract must be in writing and signed by all parties.

    a)    Brokers can assist the parties in creating such amendments.

### G.    Addenda

1.    Additional material **attached** to and made part of the initial agreement—**offer.**

    a)    Amendments modify contracts; attachments explain items attached to offers.

**IV.   ESSENTIAL ELEMENTS OF A VALID CONTRACT**

**A.   Competent parties/contractual capacity**

1.   Age of majority is 18; a contract with a minor is **voidable**.

2.   Mentally sound—contract with someone declared incompetent by a court is **void**. That person can enter a contract **only** if court appoints a guardian to act on the person's behalf.

**B.   Mutual agreement/meeting of the minds/offer and acceptance**

1.   Offer and communication of acceptance must be made before the offer has been withdrawn.

   a)   Offer may be withdrawn by either party prior to communication of acceptance to the party who made the offer.

   b)   **Qualified acceptance or counteroffer is <u>rejection and terminates the original offer</u>.**

   c)   If counteroffer is initialed by both parties, it is accepted.

   d)   A buyer who receives a counteroffer is not obligated to respond and may make an offer on a new property without obligation to the seller that countered the first offer.

   e)   A seller who counters and then receives an offer from another party must withdraw the counteroffer before accepting the new offer.

**C.   Lawful objective/legal purpose**

**D.   Consideration/money or something of value**

1.   Not earnest money (which is not required)

**E.   In writing and signed (certain contracts, based on statute of frauds)**

**V.   STATUTE OF FRAUDS AND STATUTE OF LIMITATIONS**

**A.   Statute of frauds requires that agreements be in writing**

1.   The statute of frauds requires that certain contracts for the transfer of real estate be in writing to be enforceable.

2.   **The law does NOT apply to leases of 12 months or less.**

**B.   Purpose of statute of frauds**

1.   To prevent problems with oral real estate contracts

**C.   Statute of limitations**

1.   Sets the length of time parties will be given to file a claim or lawsuit

## VI.   TYPES OF REAL ESTATE CONTRACTS

### A.   Purchase agreement/offer to purchase/contract of sale

1. The agreement is bilateral—promise for a promise.

2. Offer becomes a valid and binding contract when acceptance is communicated.

3. It is executory until performance by parties (closing).

4. Buyer (vendee) has <u>equitable title and is the equitable owner</u>; seller (vendor) has <u>legal title and is the legal owner</u>.

5. The agreement may include a **contingency clause** allowing the buyer to terminate under certain conditions (e.g., buyer would get earnest money back) if he cancels per the terms.

   a) The most typical contingency is for financing.

      (1) If the buyer terminates the contract per a contingency, the buyer's earnest money is returned.

   b) Brokers are **not paid** if a contract terminates per a contingency.

6. Earnest money is **not** consideration and is not required to create a valid purchase agreement.

### B.   Option

1. Owner/seller gives buyer the right to buy for **a set price and set term**.

2. Option fee is paid by buyer for the right.

3. Owner/seller retains option fee if buyer decides not to buy.

4. Unilateral contract; becomes bilateral when option exercised by buyer.

5. **Unlike a bilateral, installment, or land contract, if the buyer decided not to purchase, the seller who gave the option would have no recourse against the buyer.**

### C.   Lease purchase

1. Lease purchase is two contracts: a purchase agreement and a lease.

2. Portion of lease payments can be applied to a down payment.

## VII.   REMEDIES FOR BREACH OF CONTRACT/DEFAULT

### A.   Mutual rescission

1. Mutual rescission is the mutual agreement of all parties to <u>cancel</u> all obligations.

   a) It returns all parties to their original condition before the contract was executed.

b)  The buyer's earnest money is returned.

c)  **It would be acceptable if there are major problems** (e.g., the house burns down or there are many repair items).

d)  **It would <u>not</u> be acceptable** if the buyer decides she doesn't like the house or wants to buy a different property.

## B. Remedies for default

1.  Enforce specific performance (court action to force breaching party to perform)

    a)  Specific performance is the only option, per the contract, for the buyer if the seller decides to terminate.

2.  Terminate the contract and receive earnest money as <u>liquidated damages</u>, thereby releasing both parties from contract

3.  Sue for actual damages

# Practice of Real Estate

(Test questions: Salesperson 12; Broker 12)

**I.    CIVIL RIGHTS ACT OF 1866**

    **A.  Prohibits discrimination based on race or ancestry**

**II.    FEDERAL FAIR HOUSING ACT OF 1968 AND ITS AMENDMENTS**

    **A.  Protected classifications (memory aid: FReSH CoRN)**

       1.  Family status (added in 1988)

         a)  Protects pregnant women and families with children

         b)  **Does <u>not</u> apply to retirement communities in which 80% of the units are occupied by residents age 55 or older**

       2.  Race (only protected class in the 1866 Civil Rights Act)

       3.  Sex (added in 1974)

       4.  Handicap/disability (added in 1988)—any physical or mental impairment that **substantially limits** one or more major life activity

         a)  It includes those suffering from HIV/AIDS.

         b)  Alcoholics and drug addicts are protected if seeking treatment, but are not protected if using illegal drugs.

           (1)  Law specifically excludes those convicted of dealing drugs.

           (2)  Landlords are not obligated to rent to a person with a history of violence.

         c)  Both current and recovered mental patients are protected.

         d)  Landlords must allow disabled tenants to make changes at the tenant's expense. The owner may require the tenant to return the property to its original condition upon termination of the lease.

       5.  Color

       6.  Religion

       7.  National origin

    **B.  Not protected under federal law**

       1.  Age

       2.  Sexual orientation

3. Marital status

4. Occupation (e.g., student)

## C. Prohibited actions

1. **Steering**—the **channeling** of potential buyers to or away from particular areas as a means of discrimination

2. **Blockbusting**, also called panic peddling—inducing people to sell their homes because of the entry into the neighborhood of members of protected classes

3. **Redlining**—refusing to offer or limiting loans in certain areas; **may not refuse to loan based on high crime rates in a neighborhood**

4. Less favorable treatment

5. Discriminatory or restrictive advertising

## D. Exceptions—apply to the person, not the property

1. **There are no exceptions in regard to racial discrimination.** It is not a violation to discriminate against other protected classifications in the following situations:

   a) Rental or sale of a single-family home (no broker involvement and no discriminatory advertising)

   b) Rental of units (four-unit building or less) where the owner occupies one of the units (no broker involvement and no discriminatory advertising)

   c) Nonprofit organizations may restrict to members only.

   d) Rental or sale of units in buildings with at least **80% of occupants age 55+. Senior housing exemption: may discriminate against families with children—familial status.**

## E. Complaints

1. **HUD will first investigate all incidents.**

   a) Complaints can be filed with HUD within one year of the discriminatory act.

   b) Aggrieved party can file civil suit directly **in federal court within two years**.

2. A broker could file a complaint and request the commission as damages if a seller refuses to accept an offer from a protected class.

3. A broker's best protection is to keep good records.

4. When advertising, it is best to describe the property, not who should or should not live there.

5.  In a complaint, HUD will consider the following:

    a)  Testing studies done on the company by HUD

    b)  The properties shown to the buyer or tenant

    c)  If an equal opportunity poster is displayed in the office

6.  HUD will not consider the broker or salesperson's intentions even if the broker/salesperson felt he was working in the buyer's best interest (e.g., showing only neighborhoods with children to a family).

## III.  EQUAL CREDIT OPPORTUNITY ACT (ECOA)

### A.  Prohibits discrimination in all consumer credit transactions based on the following:

1.  Race, religion, color, sex, and national origin

2.  Prohibits lenders from refusing loans to the following qualified borrowers:

    a)  **Age—must lend to retired persons**

    b)  Marital status—may not deny if unmarried

    c)  Public assistance/income—may not deny if receiving and can qualify

    d)  **Remember AMP: A**ge, **M**arital status, and **P**ublic assistance

### B.  Does <u>NOT</u> protect minors, a person's sexual orientation, or people with erratic employment histories

### C.  Requires the lender to give notice of why credit was refused

## IV.  AMERICANS WITH DISABILITIES ACT (ADA)

### A.  Purpose

1.  Ensures equal access to **public** accommodations for disabled persons

    a)  Public accommodations are places accessible to the public (including a broker's office and retail stores).

## V.  MEGAN'S LAW

### A.  Megan's Law requires the registration of sex offenders.

### B.  Brokers should inform buyers who may be concerned about a registered sex offender to contact local law enforcement offices.

### C.  States vary on the requirements of brokers for disclosure and how to inform buyers of this law.

## VI.    THE OBLIGATIONS OF THE BROKERAGE FIRM

### A.  The brokerage firm

1. The brokerage firm owns all contracts and has the agency relationship. When salespersons and broker associates leave the firm, they may not take contracts or listings without permission.

2. The employing broker (responsible/principal broker or broker in charge) is responsible for the following:

    a) **All contracts**, listings (employment), and purchase agreements

    b) Supervising all licensees under them

### B.  Role of salesperson or broker associate

1. Employed to represent the broker and brokerage firm

    a) **Owe duties to the client equivalent to the duties owed by the employing broker**

2. Can be an employee or independent contractor

    a) **For employees,** brokers **must withhold taxes** but do not have to guarantee vacations, set schedules, or require them to work set hours.

    b) **Independent contractors must have a <u>written signed agreement</u> that states they <u>may set their own work hours</u>** and pay their own taxes.

## VII.    ETHICS FOR REAL ESTATE PROFESSIONALS

■  Ethics refers to a system of moral principles, rules, and standards of conduct.

### A.  Expectations of brokers and salespeople

1. Exhibit a higher level of knowledge and competency than a nonlicensed individual.

2. Protect the interests of clients and treat all parties fairly and honestly.

3. Complete all state-mandated disclosures in a timely fashion.

4. Fully explain to the client the obligations of the client and broker in the transaction.

### B.  Disclosure and practicing within levels of competence

1. All real estate professionals are expected to know when they are not competent to perform a task, including:

    a) Practicing outside their area of expertise (e.g., residential broker selling commercial property, city broker selling farm land)

b)   Completing and presenting legal documents that are not fully understood by the broker

c)   A salesperson or broker becomes competent by completing education and working with others who are knowledgeable in the area of practice.

2.   A real estate professional is expected to fully disclose:

a)   Who they represent in the transaction

b)   Obligations of all parties in regard to disclosure of material defects

c)   Whether she is a principal in the transaction

d)   Any environmental, material, or other issues requiring disclosure that might impact the property

## C.  Illegal practice of law

1.   Real estate professionals must know when they need to recommend that the party they are working with should seek legal advice.

2.   Broker associates and salespeople should recommend the use of attorneys, accountants, and other appropriate counsel to both buyers and sellers.

3.   A licensee is not allowed to give legal advice on any aspect of the real estate transaction.

## D.  National Do Not Call Registry

1.   National list of phone numbers telemarketers cannot call

a)   Real estate brokers and salespeople must check the list before cold calling.

2.   Brokers may contact consumers for three months after they have made an inquiry.

3.   Brokers may call consumers with whom they have an established business relationship for up to 18 months after the last purchase.

# VIII.   BROKER'S TRUST ACCOUNTS

## A.  Broker's trust account defined

1.   Broker's trust accounts are accounts with funds held <u>for others</u> by the brokerage firm—for example, **earnest money**, tax and insurance, escrow payment, and unearned commissions.

## B.  Handling earnest money

1.   Deposits

a)   Licensee must give earnest money checks to listing brokerage firm immediately after the offer is accepted.

b)   Managing or employing broker of the listing firm *must deposit the funds* in a trust account.

    (1)   **Trust accounts must be demand accounts that allow for free deposit and withdrawal of funds.**

    (2)   Time limit for depositing earnest money is set by state law.

c)   **If the broker receives a NSF (not sufficient funds) check, the broker must immediately inform the seller.**

2.   Commingling is prohibited; brokers cannot mix personal funds with trust funds.

3.   Using trust funds for personal reasons or for other people is called conversion.

4.   Broker must keep accurate records of all money deposited in and disbursed from the trust account.

# Financing

**(Test questions: Salesperson 6; Broker 7)**

**I.   TITLE THEORY VERSUS LIEN THEORY**

   **A.  In title theory states, the borrower gives legal title to the lender. Typically, the title is held by a third party trustee (often a public trustee).**

   **B.  In lien theory states, the mortgagor retains legal title and gives the mortgagee a lien as security for the debt.**

**II.   FINANCING INSTRUMENTS**

   **A.  Promissory note**

      1.  Promise to repay and terms; evidence of the debt

      2.  Features may include the following:

         a)  Prepayment clause—privilege to prepay

         b)  **Acceleration clause—speeds up the note when the borrower is in default**

      3.  Secured by a mortgage or deed of trust

   **B.  Mortgage and deed of trust (security instruments)**

      1.  Contract that pledges property as security for repayment without giving up possession

      2.  Includes the following covenants—causes of foreclosure and default:

         a)  Nonpayment of principal and interest

         b)  Nonpayment of taxes

         c)  Inadequate or no insurance

         d)  Waste

         e)  **Due-on-sale clause/alienation**

            (1)  Stops assumption without lender's consent

            (2)  Allows the lender to accelerate the loan if the borrower sells the property without paying off the loan

      3.  Includes acceleration clause, which allows the lender to demand immediate payment of entire balance owed if the mortgage is in default

      4.  Mortgage is a two-party instrument:

         a)  Borrower = mortgagor

         b)  Lender = mortgagee

5. Deed of trust is a three-party instrument:

   a) Trustor = borrower

   b) Beneficiary = lender

   c) Trustee = third party

## C. Satisfaction (defeasance)

1. When mortgage note is paid, mortgagee gives satisfaction to release lien.

2. When deed of trust is paid, trustee gives deed of reconveyance to release lien.

## III.    FORECLOSURE

### A. Foreclosure is a legal procedure whereby property used as security for a debt is taken by a <u>creditor</u> or is sold to pay off the debt.

1. **Insufficient proceeds from a foreclosure sale could result in a deficiency or personal judgment, not a default judgment.**

2. Foreclosure laws are implemented at a state level.

3. **A foreclosure removes all liens from the property.**

### B. Deed in lieu of foreclosure

1. Alternative to foreclosure—mortgagor deeds to mortgagee

2. Lender does not have to accept

3. Disadvantage to lender—**does not** wipe out secondary liens

   a) **If lender accepts a deed in lieu of foreclosure, then the lender would take title subject to any junior liens**

### C. Short sales

1. Short sales occur when a seller is in default prior to foreclosure.

2. The broker lists the property for sale, often at a price lower than what is owed on the loan.

3. Once an offer is received, the lender may agree to accept the reduced (deficient) price.

4. The lender may require seller to pay any deficiency, and the seller may have tax consequences.

**IV.   METHODS OF DEBT REPAYMENT/DEBT SERVICE**

### A.  Term/straight/interest-only loan

1. **Interest only** is paid until maturity at end of term.

2. Loan has a small monthly payment, but a large balloon.

3. The full amount of principal (balloon) is **due at the end.**

### B.  Partially amortized

1. Repaid in equal payments of <u>principal</u> and interest

2. Larger payment than a term loan but smaller than a fully amortized loan

3. **Has a balloon payment at the end of the term that will be smaller than the original loan amount**

### C.  Fully amortized

1. **Loan is repaid in equal payments of principal and interest with the balance paid in full on the last payment so there is no balloon.**

2. Payments, which are larger than a term or partially amortized loan, are made at regular intervals.

3. Interest is paid in arrears.

### D.  Adjustable-rate mortgage (ARM)

1. Rate subject to change based on changes in an economic index

2. May include interest and/or payment caps

3. **Interest rate = Index + Margin (e.g., 5% index + 2% margin = 7% interest)**

### E.  Budget (PITI)

1. The borrower pays P&I plus 1/12 taxes and 1/12 insurance into the lender's impound escrow account (interest and taxes are deductible).

2. The lender will always collect for the month of closing. A house closing in March would have 3 months of impounds in the escrow account (January, February, and March).

### F.  Reverse mortgage

1. Mortgagee makes payments to mortgagor over a specific term.

2. Used to obtain money from the equity in the home when a senior does not want to sell but needs cash.

3. Is due upon sale of the property, death of mortgagor(s), or at the end of the term.

### G. Line of credit

1. Allows the borrower to obtain further advances at a later date

2. Future advance limited to the difference between original loan amount and current amount owed

### H. Subprime loans

1. Borrower is of higher risk, so the loan is more likely to default.

2. A higher-than-prime rate is charged because the borrower and/or the property used as security is a **higher risk than a prime borrower** (e.g., prime rate might be 6% and subprime would be 8%).

## V.   SELLER FINANCING

### A. Contract for deed/land contract/installment contract

1. **Seller (vendor) who retains legal title <u>holds the deed</u>; buyer (vendee) has equitable title.**

2. Buyer takes possession when the contract is signed.

3. **Seller transfers title via a deed when the buyer makes the final payment.**

### B. Seller carry-back purchase money

1. Owner financing where title transfers to the buyer

2. Seller takes back a mortgage as partial payment; seller has lien

### C. With seller financing, real estate professionals should make sure both the seller and the buyer understand the risks that may be involved.

## VI.   MISCELLANEOUS MORTGAGE TERMS

### A. LTV (loan-to-value ratio/mortgage ratio)

1. Maximum percentage of value the lender will loan

2. **Used to determine loan amount and if the borrower will have to pay PMI**

3. **Based on price or appraisal, whichever is less**

### B. Equity

1. **Market value today – Total debt today = Equity**

### C. Points and loan origination fee

1. Discount points are charged by the lender to increase lender's yield (1 point = 1% of loan amount).

2. Loan origination fee is charged by the lender to process and issue a loan.

3. **Both are tax deductible.**

### D. Leverage

1. Borrowed money is used to increase investment return.

2. It does not give more equity and requires a small down payment.

3. The advantage is that the borrower can control a large asset with very little cash.

   a) Example: $100,000 loan for a $10,000 cash down payment

4. The disadvantage is the **higher risk** created by less equity (e.g., the lower the equity, the higher the risk of the borrower defaulting).

### E. Other clauses

1. A **subordination** clause allows a change in the order/priority of mortgages.

2. **Usury** is the charging of an interest rate in excess of what is permitted by state law.

   a) State laws determine the **maximum interest rate** limits and the type of loans affected by usury law.

## VII. CONVENTIONAL/INSURED CONVENTIONAL LOANS

### A. Loans are not insured or guaranteed by the government. They often require PMI insurance.

1. Depending on loan-to-value ratio, lender may require private mortgage insurance (PMI).

   a) **Loans over 80% LTV require PMI.**

   b) PMI does not payoff the full loan amount.

2. The advantage to the borrower is a smaller down payment.

## VIII. GOVERNMENT PROGRAMS

■ Funds come from qualified lenders approved by HUD.

### A. <u>FHA</u> (Federal Housing Administration)—<u>insures</u> lenders against loss due to foreclosure

B. <u>VA</u> (Department of Veterans Affairs)—<u>guarantees</u> lenders against loss on loans to veterans

1. Up to 100% loan-to-value ratio is allowed.

2. **Individuals must be veterans, active National Guard members, or retired military reserve members.**

   a) Parents of veterans are not eligible.

C. Miscellaneous aspects of FHA/VA

1. Rules regarding assumption depend on the date of the original loan.

2. **No prepayment penalty is allowed, no matter when or how the loan was originated.**

3. Nonveterans may assume VA loans.

4. **Borrowers must have an appraisal** to be approved for the first loan.

5. Both offer **higher loan-to-value ratios** than conventional mortgages.

## IX. SOURCES OF LOAN MONEY

A. Primary mortgage market—mortgage bankers and mortgage brokers

1. Mortgage brokers act as an **intermediary between borrowers and lenders but don't usually service loans.**

2. Mortgage bankers originate and service loans with **their company's money.**

B. Predatory lending—umbrella term for unfair or illegal lending practices

1. Predatory lending often occurred in the subprime market.

2. Many states now have predatory lending laws that require lenders and originators to be licensed.

3. Subprime loans were often coupled with down payment assistance (second mortgage) in which borrowers made no down payment and borrowed 100%. This made these loans more likely to default.

C. Secondary mortgage market

1. **Buys mortgages** from primary lenders, which are **banks, not retirement or insurance funds**, to supplement the mortgage and lending process

2. Borrowers may need to send monthly payments to a new address if their mortgage is sold

3. The following are organizations that sell mortgage-backed securities to investors:

   a) **FNMA—buys all types of mortgages** (Federal National Mortgage Association or Fannie Mae)

   b) GNMA—an agency of HUD; backs FHA/VA mortgages (Government National Mortgage Association or Ginnie Mae)

   c) FHLMC—buys from S&L's and commercial banks (Federal Home Loan Mortgage Corporation or Freddie Mac)

## X.    FINANCING/CREDIT LAWS

### A.  Truth in Lending Act—Federal Reserve Board regulates

1. **Purpose**—promotes the informed use of consumer credit by requiring disclosures about its terms and cost

2. Disclosure requirements—<u>shows the true cost of credit = APR</u>

   a) <u>**Lender finance charges**</u> **(loan origination fees, interest, discount points, and assumption fees) must be disclosed.**

   b) Annual percentage rate (APR) is the effective rate that includes the **note rate plus the total cost of credit. APR will be higher than the note rate.**

   c) **Three-day right of rescission allows the borrower to withdraw from loans on home improvements and refinances.**

      (1) **It is not used when purchasing a first home or a vacation home, or when using a construction loan.**

3. Advertising requirements—general terms are okay

   a) Price and/or APR are the only specific finance terms allowed in advertisements without disclosing all terms.

   b) Down payment, interest rate, monthly payments, or number of payments **trigger full disclosure.**

### B.  RESPA—Real Estate Settlement Procedures Act

1. Lender must give "Guide to Settlement Costs" booklet and a <u>**good-faith estimate of all closing costs**</u> at time of application or no later than <u>**3 days after**</u>

   a) Closing expenses, legal fees, and title insurance premiums are not finance charges but are disclosed under RESPA.

   b) Broker's commission is not included.

2. Borrower has right to inspect Uniform Settlement Statement (HUD-1) 1 day before closing

3. Restricts amount of advance escrow payments for taxes and insurance—no more than 3 months plus what is owed

4. **Remember**

   a) <u>Truth in Lending</u> = true cost of credit and <u>lender costs</u>

   b) <u>RESPA</u> = disclosure of <u>all closing costs</u> within 3 days

# 5

# Valuation and Market Analysis

**(Test questions: Salesperson 8; Broker 6)**

# I. APPRAISAL

## A. Defined

1. An *estimate or opinion* of market <u>value</u>, done by a licensed appraiser

   a) Regulated at both a state and federal level

2. **Required for all federally related loan programs such as FHA, VA, or conventional loans**

   a) Not required for cash or seller carry loans

## B. Licensing

1. Appraisers must be licensed or certified according to state law and in accordance with federal regulations.

2. **Appraisers may have further designations, such as MAI or SRA, from the Appraisal Institute.**

## C. Competitive market analysis (CMA)/Broker's price opinion (BPO)/Broker's opinion of value (BOV)

1. A real estate professional's job is to perform a CMA. Real estate professionals may charge a fee, but they must make sure the CMA is not mistaken for an appraisal.

2. <u>The CMA/BPO/BOV assists both the seller and the buyer</u> in determining value, but it **may not be used to finance property.**

# II. VALUE

■ The best way for sellers to determine the value of their property is to have an appraisal. If this is not a choice, then they should get a CMA, especially prior to listing, even if the broker thinks she knows the value.

## A. Market value—<u>the most probable price</u> in terms of cash or its equivalent that a property will bring

## B. Market price

1. The actual price paid in a transaction

## C. Essential elements or characteristics of value (DUST)

1. Demand

2. Utility (usefulness)

3. Scarcity

4. Transferability

## D. Principles of value

1. Highest and best use

   a) Produces greatest net return over time

   b) Is not necessarily present use

   c) **Must show current <u>highest and best use</u> in an appraisal, which <u>would NOT</u> be included in a CMA**

2. Substitution

   a) If several similar properties are for sale, lowest-priced property has the greatest demand

   b) <u>**Underlies all approaches to value—especially sales comparison approach**</u>

3. Supply and demand

   a) **Supply and demand sets rental and listing prices.**

   b) Supply—amount of properties available. Prices move opposite supply. If there is a large quantity of properties for sale or rent, prices go down.

   c) Demand—amount of properties that will be purchased. Prices move with demand. If properties are scarce and desired, prices go up.

4. Contribution—value of improvement based on increasing or decreasing return

   a) Increasing—improvements add more value than cost.

   b) Decreasing—improvements add less value than cost.

5. Conformity

   a) Values tend to move toward surroundings.

   b) Regression—value of over improved property declines.

   c) Progression—value of under improved property increases.

## III.    METHODS OF ESTIMATING VALUE/APPRAISAL PROCESS

### A.    Sales comparison approach—primarily residential

1.    *Subject* is the property being evaluated—**never adjust the subject property.**

2.    *Comparables* or *comps* are recently sold similar properties.

3.    Adjustments are made to comparables—adjust to make *like subject*:

a)    If comparable feature is better than subject, subtract.

b)    If comparable feature is worse than subject, add.

c)    Market cycles often create the need for a *time of sale* or *days on market* adjustment.

(1)    Might adjust for date of sale in an appreciating or depreciating market

(2)    **Use the most current comparables in a rapidly changing market; preferably within 6 months but no longer than 1 year**

d)    **Adjust for date of sale, location, and square footage, but NOT for capitalization (which is used in the income approach).**

4.    Value of the item being adjusted is determined by comparing properties with and without the item.

a)    For example, the value of a fireplace or air conditioning would be determined by the differences between the sales of comparable homes with and without a fireplace or air conditioning.

5.    **Obtaining an appraisal or CMA is the best way to determine the market value of a property.**

### B.    Cost approach/summation approach—most effective method for new construction and special-purpose or single-purpose buildings

■    Cost to build new—Accrued depreciation + Land value = Estimated value

1.    **Estimate new construction cost**

a)    **Reproduction cost new—replica with same or highly similar materials**

b)    **Replacement cost new—same function or utility**

### C.    Income approach—income-producing properties, such as apartments, office buildings, or shopping centers

1.    Capitalization—conversion of future income to present value (see Figure 5.1)

2. Calculating net operating income (NOI):

   Potential gross income *minus* Vacancy and credit loss = Effective gross income (EGI)

   EGI (effective gross income) *minus* Operating expenses = Net operating income (NOI)

3. Gross rent multiplier, or GRM (alternative to capitalization that takes into account gross income but not expenses) (See Figure 5.2.)

**FIGURE 5.1**

**IRV Circle Formula**

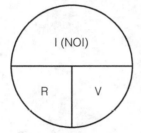

Income (net operating income) = Cap rate × Present Value

**FIGURE 5.2**

**GRM Circle Formula**

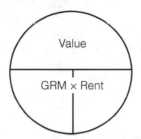

**To determine the GRM, divide the value by the monthly or annual rents.**

Formulas:

Annual gross rent multiplier × Annual gross rent = Value

OR

Monthly gross rent multiplier × Monthly gross rent = Value

OR

**Value ÷ Rents = GRM**

HINT: If you are given a problem to solve, make sure you match the time periods (e.g., annual GRM and monthly rent times 12). **A big number like 150 will be a monthly gross rent multiplier.**

## D.  Reconciliation process

1. Final step in valuation process—used to weigh the three approaches to determine the final value.

2. Appraiser analyzes and weighs estimates of value from market, cost, and income approaches.

3. Appraiser arrives at a final estimate of value, **<u>NOT</u> an average** of the value estimates.

# Property Ownership

**(Test questions: Salesperson 7; Broker 6)**

## I.   CLASSES OF PROPERTY/REAL ESTATE AND PERSONAL PROPERTY

**A.  Real estate—includes land plus improvements and appurtenances, which include rights, privileges, and fixtures**

1.  Land

a)  Surface rights

b)  Air rights

c)  Subsurface rights, including mineral rights

2.  Improvements

a)  Items affixed to the land with the intent of being permanent (a house, garage, fence, landscaping, etc.)

3.  **Appurtenances**, including rights, privileges, and fixtures

a)  Fixtures are items attached to improvements with the **intent** to become real estate as evidenced by any of the following:

(1)  **Attachment or Annexation**

(2)  **Adaptation**

(3)  **Agreement**

b)  Fixtures are part of the real estate and transfer with the property unless the contract **excludes them**.

(1)  **For example, plumbing or electrical fixtures**

(2)  **Sellers that remove fixtures, without excluding them in the contract, are in breach of contract.**

(3)  **Remember: free-standing = personal property; built-in = fixture**

c)  EXCEPTIONS: Emblements (crops) and trade fixtures are **personal property; neither would <u>automatically</u> transfer with the property.**

(1)  Emblements are annually cultivated crops that belong to the party who rightfully planted the seed.

(2)  Trade fixtures are tenant-installed additions to a property for use in a trade or business.

d)  **Land cannot be a fixture.**

**B. Personal property/chattel—everything that is not real estate**

    1. To transfer in the bill of sale, it must be <u>included</u> in the purchase agreement.

    2. **If not included in writing,** the seller may take the personal property even if it was listed in the MLS.

    3. **An example of personal property is a freestanding refrigerator.**

## II. LAND CHARACTERISTICS

### A. Physical characteristics of land

    1. Immobile, indestructible, and unique location

### B. Economic characteristics of land

    1. Scarcity, placement of improvements, and area preference

    2. Disadvantage to owning real estate is that **land lacks liquidity**

## III. LEGAL DESCRIPTION

### A. Methods of legal description

    1. Metes and bounds—description using directions and **compass degrees**

        a) Starts and ends at point of beginning (POB)—referenced from a monument

        b) Measure clockwise

            (1) **For example, "<u>Commencing or starting</u> at the street sign at the corner of Ridge and Ash, go 100 feet south and then go 100 feet west."**

    2. Rectangular survey/government survey

        a) Uses meridians, townships, ranges, tiers, and sections to locate land parcels

        b) Townships—each township contains 36 sections

        c) Section—640 acres or 1 mile by 1 mile

        d) **Acre—43,560 square feet**

    3. Recorded plat (lot, block, subdivision)—**urban/residential**

        a) First step in development is to create plat map.

        b) Second step is to **record the map.**

        c) Recording is done prior to obtaining building permits.

**FIGURE 6.1**

**Township Map**

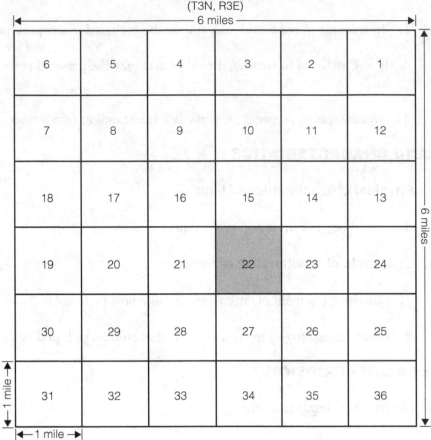

Township 3 North, Range 3 East
(T3N, R3E)

A township is divided into 36 sections.
Each section is 1 mile × 1 mile.

## B. Survey

1. A survey is an onsite measurement of property lines and the position of the property improvements and easements.

2. It is used to create or verify a legal description.

3. It uses **monuments, which are markers used to help establish property** <u>boundaries.</u>

4. It may reveal **encroachments** or zoning violations.

## C. Improvement location certificate/title survey

1. It is similar to a survey but only locates improvements on the lot. It will find **encroachments.**

## IV. TYPES OF OWNERSHIP—ESTATES AND ENCUMBRANCES

### A. Freehold estates—<u>indefinite duration</u> of ownership

1. Fee simple absolute lasts forever and features the **maximum rights of ownership.**

2. Qualified fee/fee simple defeasible lasts "so long as" **deed condition** is met.

   a) **Holder of reversionary interest would have the right to try and acquire title if the condition is broken.**

3. In a life estate, <u>life tenants have ownership</u> and use of the property for the duration of their life or the pur autre vie life.

   a) **Upon the death of the life tenant, the holder of either the reversionary or remainder interest will own a fee simple absolute estate at death.**

   b) Pur autre vie—a life estate may be based on the life of someone other than the holder of the life estate.

## B. Leasehold (nonfreehold) estates

1. Elements

   a) <u>**Have a definite duration and may be terminated**</u>.

   b) Tenant (lessee) holds a leasehold estate; landlord (lessor) holds a leased fee estate.

   c) If estate for years or periodic tenancy, a new buyer will be "subject to the lease" with tenant in possession until the lease expires.

2. Types

   a) Estate/tenancy for years—has a predetermined termination date; definite period with no notice.

   b) Periodic estate/tenancy—renews from period to period, such as month to month with the same terms and conditions upon payment of rent, until notice is given.

   c) Estate/tenancy at will—continues until terminated by the owner or tenant. Tenancy is at the owner's consent.

   d) Estate/tenancy at sufferance—occurs when a "holdover tenant" stays beyond termination without consent. If the landlord accepts payments, it becomes a periodic tenancy. It is the <u>lowest estate</u>.

## C. Encumbrances/imperfections—clouds on title may impair or lessen owner's rights. An encumbrance is a nonpossessory interest in the lands of another.

1. Easement—<u>**right to use land**</u>

   a) Right to use lands of another for a specific purpose

      (1) May or may not be paid for

      (2) Must be in writing

(3) <u>Not revocable once given</u>

(4) <u>Transfers with the land at closing unless released by the holder</u>

b) Types of easements

(1) Appurtenant easement has a dominant tenement and a servient tenement.

(2) Easement in gross has no dominant tenement, only servient (e.g., utility easement).

(3) **Easement by necessity** may be granted to a homeowner to avoid landlocked property.

(a) **NOTE: This easement is available to private owners, not to government, utility, telephone, or gas companies.**

c) Terminated by merger, release, or abandonment

2. Lien—claim that attaches to and is binding on property to secure debt repayment

a) **Property tax/special assessments lien: specific lien. Takes priority over all other liens, even those previously recorded such as a mortgage.**

b) Mechanic's lien: specific lien

c) Mortgage lien: specific lien

d) Condominium/townhouse association assessments lien: specific lien

e) Judgment or IRS lien: general lien, which attaches to all real and personal property

3. Encroachment—unauthorized use of another person's land

a) Survey points out or ILC (improvement location certificate) will find.

b) Title insurance or attorney's opinion won't protect (visual inspection).

4. **License—<u>revocable</u> permission** to use the land of another without creating an estate in land and may or may not be paid for

5. Lis pendens—recorded document that gives constructive notice of a pending lawsuit regarding title

## V.    FORMS OF OWNERSHIP

■ **An attorney for the buyer best determines the appropriate form of ownership. Licensees should NEVER advise on how to take title.**

### A. Sole ownership/estate in severalty

1. When property is owned solely and separately by one person or one entity, it is called an estate in severalty.

2. Partnerships take title in severalty.

    a) General partnership

        (1) All partners share equal profits and liability.

    b) Limited partnership

        (1) General partner is responsible for liability of investment.

        (2) **Limited partner is responsible only for the amount of his investment; limited partner's liability equals the amount invested.**

## B. Concurrent/multiple ownership

1. Tenants in common—co-ownership with <u>no</u> right of survivorship

    a) Interests passed to **heirs or devisees** upon death

    b) If no form of ownership indicated, law presumes tenancy in common

    c) May have unequal shares of ownership

    d) **Each tenant responsible for the taxes as an individual or as a group**

2. **Joint tenants—<u>co-ownership with the right of survivorship</u>**

    a) **Interests pass to co-owners/cotenants upon death without going through probate**

    b) **Overrides a will**

    c) Four unities of title—<u>P</u>ossession, <u>I</u>nterest, <u>T</u>ime, and <u>T</u>itle (PITT) required in some states

3. Tenancy by the entirety

    a) Applies exclusively to married couples in some states

## C. Common interest ownership properties

1. Condominiums and town houses

    a) Condos and town houses are real estate, portions of which are designated for separate ownership (units) and the remainder of which—**including the physical structure**—is designated for common ownership and use (common elements).

        (1) Common elements are owned by all current property owners as **tenants in common.**

    b) **Purchasers own and finance their own units.**

    c) Properties/units are transferred by deed.

    d) Each unit and its common element percentage is taxed as a separate parcel.

2. Cooperatives

    a) **Cooperative ownership is ownership of the building by a corporation**, which in turn leases space to shareholders who own stock in the corporation.

    b) **Buyers receive corporate bylaws, shares of stock, and a proprietary lease for their unit and their share of the common elements.**

    c) **Because there is no ownership of the unit, the buyer does not receive a deed.**

    d) The owner pays assessments and association fees.

    e) Just as in a condominium association, owners may have to get permission from the other owners to sell their unit (first right of refusal).

3. Time-shares

    a) A time-share is a common interest ownership form in which multiple owners have interest in a property for a certain period each year.

    b) Time-shares are most commonly used for resort-type properties.

# Land-Use Controls and Regulations

**(Test questions: Salesperson 5; Broker 5)**

## I.   GOVERNMENT'S RIGHTS IN LAND (PETE)

### A.  Police power

1. Enacts and enforces laws governing **land use**—public control of land.

2. Examples include zoning, building codes, planning, and safety codes.

3. Enforced by requiring building permits, building inspections, **certificates of occupancy**, and so forth.

### B.  Eminent domain

1. **Eminent domain is the right to "take" private land for public use.**

2. **Condemnation is the <u>process</u>.**

3. Fair compensation includes property value plus damages.

4. **Inverse condemnation**—an owner initiates a court action seeking the government to pay fair compensation when her property has been substantially interfered with.

### C.  Collect property taxes and special assessments

1. Property taxes

   a) Ad valorem (at assessed value) **taxes are based on assessed value, not on current market value.**

   b) Tax rate may be expressed as mill rate, percentage rate, or decimal.

   c) Typically, properties are reassessed on an annual basis. Property owners that believe the assessment is incorrect may **appeal to an <u>Assessor's appeal board</u>.**

2. **Special assessments—lien against specific properties that benefit from a public improvement**

   a) Paid with property taxes and enforced by a lien.

   b) **Reading the assessment roll will tell if there is a special assessment lien on the property.**

3. **Property taxes and special assessments—take priority over other liens**

### D.  Escheat

1. Government's reversionary right

   a) Abandoned property or property of intestate owners with no heirs may revert to the government.

## II.   GOVERNMENT CONTROLS BASED IN POLICE POWER—ZONING, ETC.

### A.   Zoning controls, set at a local level

1. **Master plan is used to <u>control growth</u>.**

2. **Zoning determines type of use**—residential, commercial, industrial/manufacturing, agricultural, or mixed.

    a)   Special land types include floodplains, coastal preservation, and other special-use classifications that may be regulated at a county, state, or federal level.

3. Buffer zone is an area of land (e.g., a park) that separates two drastically different land use zones.

4. Rezoning or amendment is a zoning change for an entire area.

5. **Nonconforming use** allows an owner to continue present use that no longer complies with current zoning (grandfathering).

    a)   Example: A retail store surrounded by residential property would have been **grandfathered** in when the zoning changed

    b)   Typically can't expand or rebuild as nonconforming use if property is destroyed

6. Setbacks—front, side, and rear restrict and limit the location of improvements in relation to the boundaries of the property.

7. **Variance** allows individual owner to vary or deviate to prevent economic hardship. **Used when an owner wants to vary from building codes or build into a setback.**

8. **Special (conditional) use** (also called a special exception)—specific type of variance allows a different use (e.g., **day care** in residential zoning).

    a)   **It allows the owner to deviate from zoning regulations, not from deed restrictions or building codes.**

    b)   **Buyers** who wish to continue the use or are not sure if a use is allowed should **check with the zoning department prior to buying.**

9. Any special-use zoning must be disclosed to buyers (e.g., tax districts or airport flight paths).

### B.   Building codes or standards, and certificates of occupancy

1. Building codes deal with structural integrity and safety of a building (e.g., minimum number of bathrooms per square foot in a commercial building).

    a)   Determine the types of construction materials that can be used.

    　　(1)   Set standards for types of materials and how they are used.

    　　(2)   Provide separate codes for plumbing, electrical, fire, and so forth.

2. Certificate of occupancy is issued when a new building is ready for occupancy—confirms that the building meets minimum standards.

## C. Environmental issues—regulated by the EPA (Environmental Protection Agency)

■ **All known environmental issues may impact value and must be disclosed by the seller and the broker or salesperson.**

1. **Asbestos**—mineral used in building that can cause respiratory disease

   a) It is harmful only if the fibers are exposed because the hazard is from inhaling the microscopic fibers.

   b) If a building is being demolished or renovated, **abatement** (removal) should be done by a licensed professional prior to demolition.

   c) **Encapsulation (sealing in place) is often a better choice** than removal because there is no danger of exposing the fibers.

2. Lead-based paint

   a) Disclosure requirements

      (1) The seller must give a copy of the **EPA pamphlet** to buyers of homes that were built **prior to January 1, 1978**.

      (2) Buyers have a 10-day opportunity to have the home tested and may **waive their right to have an inspection**.

      (3) The seller is not required to do a **lead inspection or removal**.

      (4) Lead is **not typically found in wall insulation but might be in soil, pipes, and paint**.

   b) Broker's responsibility

      (1) Real estate brokers are responsible for making sure all parties are **in compliance**.

3. **Radon—a naturally occurring odorless radioactive gas**

   a) Enters through cracks in the basement and can cause lung cancer

   b) Typically **mitigated** by adding a ventilation system to move the gas outside

   c) **Relatively inexpensive to detect and mitigate**

4. **Carbon monoxide (CO)**—odorless gas that is the by-product of combustion

   a) If combustible appliances, furnaces, and wood stoves are working properly and have proper ventilation, CO is not an issue.

   b) Many states mandate that properties must have CO detectors.

5. **Mold**—toxic mold is created by excess moisture

   a) Not all mold is hazardous; in fact, it is naturally occurring in the air. All mold requires moisture to grow.

   b) If found in walls or other areas of housing, it may be considered toxic and would require remediation.

   c) **Remediation** (removal) should be done per EPA and state regulations.

   d) There is no federal disclosure law; however, some states have disclosure requirements.

   e) All sellers must disclose if there is a mold issue.

   f) Brokers and salespeople should be aware of indications of mold, including musty smell, water damage, high humidity, and water leaks.

6. Other environmental issues

   a) Formaldehyde, chlorofluorocarbons, electromagnetic fields, and methamphetamine labs all pose potential problems.

   b) Brokers and salespeople should also be aware of the impact of underground storage tanks, groundwater pollution, brownfields, and waste disposal sites.

## D. Environmental impact statement (EIS)

1. An EIS is a report that assesses the probable impact on the environment of a <u>proposed</u> project.

2. **Environmental issues may impact value, and disclosure of the fact an EIS is being done would be required, even if the report is not finalized.**

## III.  WATER RIGHTS

### A.  Riparian rights

1. Incidental to ownership of land abutting flowing water (stream or river)

### B.  Littoral rights

1. Incidental to ownership of land abutting water that is not flowing (lake or ocean)

### C.  Doctrine of prior appropriation

1. Certain states rely on the **doctrine of <u>prior appropriation</u>**, which states that the first user diverting to **beneficial use** has the first claim on the water.

## IV.    PRIVATE CONTROLS ON LAND USE

### A.  Deed restrictions or covenants are <u>privately created controls on land use</u>.

1.  Might control style of improvement or use of property and must be legal

    a)  For example, no RVs are allowed in driveways; houses must be painted in certain colors; fencing must be of a certain type; garages must be certain shape and size; and so forth.

2.  **May not violate fair housing laws (e.g., cannot refuse to sell based on race or national origin)**

3.  Used by developers to protect property values and the interests of property owners in a subdivision

4.  Are binding on all present and future owners

5.  Property owner subject to injunction if deed restriction is violated

# Specialty Areas

**(Test questions: Salesperson 2; Broker 3)**

## I.    COMMERCIAL PROPERTY

### A.  Commercial property defined

1.  Commercial property is a classification of real estate that includes nonresidential income-producing property—**not apartments**.

a)  Commercial use requires property to be zoned for business purposes.

2.  Examples of commercial property:

a)  **Office building**, gas station, restaurant, shopping center, hotel/motel, and **parking lot**

## II.   LEASES

### A.  Types of leases

1.  Gross lease/fixed lease—tenant pays fixed rent; landlord pays all expenses (utilities, taxes, or special assessments).

a)  Typically used in residential properties but can be used for commercial or industrial properties

2.  Net lease—tenant pays fixed rent plus expenses (utilities, taxes, or special assessments); most common for commercial properties.

3.  Percentage lease—tenant pays percentage of income as rent.

4.  Index lease—rent is adjusted based on an economic index.

5.  Sale-leaseback—converts equity to capital without giving up possession.

### B.  Constructive eviction

1.  The lease may be terminated if the lessee (tenant) must vacate due to the lessor's (landlord's) act or failure to act; wrongful eviction.

### C.  Actual eviction

1.  Actual eviction is used by landlords to evict tenants who are in breach of their lease.

## III.  BUSINESS OPPORTUNITY SALES

### A.  Sale of a business, including goodwill and assets

1.  Many states require a broker's license to offer for sale for another for a fee.

# Mandated Disclosures

**(Test questions: Salesperson 8; Broker 9)**

## I. MANDATED DISCLOSURES

### A. Seller's property disclosure

1. The disclosure may be a required form or a written list.

   a) The disclosure should cover all issues that might make buyers change their decision.

2. Sellers (never the broker) complete the disclosure to the best of their **current actual knowledge**.

3. The sellers and the broker must disclose **all** material defects (facts), both visible and latent (hidden), to all buyers even if selling "as is."

### B. Material facts

1. The seller and broker/salesperson must reveal all known material facts.

   a) **Material facts first must be revealed to the party the agent represents and then to the other broker/salesperson and parties to the transaction.**

   b) **Stigmatized property requirements (e.g., disclosure of a murder) are determined by <u>state law</u>.**

   c) The broker/salesperson is not responsible for discovering latent (hidden) facts that the seller did not disclose.

2. A licensee who withholds or lies about material facts may be guilty of misrepresentation or fraud, and the contract may be voidable.

   a) Note: Puffing is an exaggerated opinion (e.g., "This is the best house on the market" or "This house has the best lake view") and does not constitute misrepresentation.

3. **A listing agent has a duty to present all offers** to the client, unless otherwise specified in writing. Multiple offers should be presented simultaneously.

   a) A broker must do as the seller requests to make sure that all parties, even third parties, are protected. **The listing broker must follow the seller's directions to prevent harm to others, especially for setting showings (e.g., if the house has a hazard that the seller warned the listing broker about, the listing broker is responsible to make sure no one enters).**

4. The buyer's ability to get a loan is considered a material fact. The buyer and buyer's agent have to disclose if the buyer is unable to get a loan.

5. Brokers owe those they don't represent honesty, fair dealing, and care, even if the principal asks them to lie or keep silent; they **must** disclose all known material facts.

   a) Note: A licensee may not inflate the sales price in hopes of securing a listing and then lowering the price later. This is an example of **unethical behavior**.

6. All environmental issues, even those outside the property boundaries, are considered to be material facts that must be disclosed because they may impact property values.

## II.   WARRANTIES—DISCLOSURE REQUIREMENTS SET BY STATE LAW

### A.  Home warranty programs for existing homes

1.  Home warranties cover most of the home, including all major systems and appliances.

2.  Home warranties are often provided as part of the listing or offer. They feature a deductible and may exclude some items from coverage.

3.  **The terms and length of the warranty are determined <u>by the contract</u> with the warranty company.**

4.  Brokers and salespeople should make sure buyers know that warranties are available.

### B.  New home construction warranties

1.  These warranties are provided on newly constructed homes by the builder and must meet strict underwriting guidelines.

2.  New home construction warranties cover failure of workmanship and material, and failures of inclusions, including **merchantability and habitability**.

   a)  **Covers roof or other structural failures after closing**

   b)  **Does not cover structural damage from outside forces**

3.  Requirements for builder warranties are set at the state or local level.

4.  Brokers should make sure buyers fully understand the limits of all warranties.

# Transfer of Title

**(Test questions: Salesperson 5; Broker 5)**

## I. DEEDS

### A. Key points

1. The purpose of a deed is to **transfer title between the owner/grantor and the receiver/grantee.**

2. A seller of real property will always be called on to provide <u>a written deed.</u>

3. The major difference between types of deeds lies in the extent of the promises given by the grantor to the grantee.

4. Deeds do not guarantee or prove ownership.

5. Deeds do <u>not</u> have to be recorded for title to transfer; title passes upon acceptance of the grantee.

### B. Types of deeds in private grants (voluntary alienation)

1. Warranty deed/general warranty deed (best for grantee)—five covenants and a guarantee of title

   a) **Covenant of seisin**—grantor has right to convey.

   b) Covenant of quiet enjoyment—grantee will not be disturbed by others.

   c) Covenant against encumbrances—there are no unspecified encumbrances.

   d) Covenant of further assurance—cooperation in signing additional documents.

   e) Warranty forever—is guarantee of defense.

2. Limited (special) warranty deed—**warrants only those defects and encumbrances that occur during the grantor's period of ownership.**

3. Quitclaim deed (best for grantor)—used as problem solver and to terminate deed restrictions; no promises, no guarantees.

   a) **For example, a seller would use a quitclaim deed after foreclosure so there would be NO future claims or liability.**

4. Bargain and sale deed—contains only implied warranties that the grantor holds the title and possessions of the property.

### C. Public grant

1. **Government transfers ownership by land patent** to private party.

### D. Essential elements of a valid deed

1. Competent grantor—age 18 and of sound mind

2. Executed by grantor(s)

3. Identifiable grantee

4. Delivered and accepted by grantee(s)—title and possession of property (unless otherwise agreed) pass at this point

5. Legal description

6. Consideration—money or something of value

7. **Words of conveyance—granting clause**

## II.    SPECIAL PROCESSES

### A.  Conveyance after death

1. Probate is the process of distributing all of a deceased's assets.

    a) **A will must go through probate for real and personal property to be distributed.**

    b) Joint tenants do **not** go through probate to claim title to the property.

2. **Devise** is the act of transferring the deceased's interest in real estate to another by will (hook to deed).

3. **Bequest** is the act of transferring a deceased's interest in personal property to another (hook to bill of sale).

4. If a person dies intestate (without a will), laws of descent and intestate succession determine heirs/descendents.

### B.  Other ways of transferring rights (involuntary alienation)

1. **Adverse possession** is ownership granted by the courts due to open, continuous, actual, notorious (hostile), and **exclusive** <u>possession</u> of another's land for a minimum statutory period.

2. **Easement by prescription/prescriptive easement** is an easement prescribed by the courts due to open, continuous, actual, and notorious (hostile) <u>use of another's land</u> for a minimum statutory period.

3. **Remember the memory aid OCEAN: possession or use must be Open (visible), Continuous, Exclusive (distinct), Actual, and Notorious (hostile).**

4. If all parties recognize, accept, and permit the possession of the property or use of the easement, it **cannot be** adverse possession or an easement by prescription.

    a) Hostile implies <u>that it is without</u> the owner's permission.

## C. Recording

1. Generally not required for validity.

2. Gives constructive (legal) notice to protect interests.

3. **Determines priority (first in time, first in right).**

   a) **A deed that is not recorded** creates the risk that a later interest could take priority and **does <u>not</u> have constructive notice of ownership.**

4. State laws govern specifics of recording and generally include the following requirements:

   a) Recorded deeds/mortgages must be executed by grantors/mortgagors.

   b) Documents must be dated.

   c) Signatures should be acknowledged (notarized)—**required in most states to record.**

      (1) Acknowledgment (notarizing) shows signature is genuine and not made under duress.

## III. TITLE INSURANCE

### A. Buyer's goal is to obtain marketable (merchantable) title

### B. Abstract with a title opinion

1. <u>Abstract of title (title abstract) is a historical summary of all conveyances</u> and encumbrances against the property.

2. Title opinion is done by an attorney after reviewing the abstract.

### C. Title insurance

1. The title examiner checks and traces chain of title for history of conveyances.

2. **Unlike an abstract, which lists historical information, the title commitment/report lists <u>current title status</u> and title defects (mortgages, easements, etc.) but no history of documents.**

   a) The title commitment/report is the promise to insure the title; it will <u>not</u> cover items listed as exceptions and defects.

3. A standard title insurance policy protects **against defects discovered in the title after closing not <u>before</u> closing.**

4. The types of policies are the following:

   a) Owner's policy: protects owner (buyer) and heirs while they have an interest

      (1) Negotiable items that the seller may provide for the new buyer

b)  Mortgagee's policy: protects lender giving them title coverage

(1)  Buyer often pays this premium for the lender.

5.  Premiums are paid once at closing. The policy is issued at or after closing.

6.  A broker who is a partner or affiliated with a title company may, **with written disclosure of the broker's relationship to the title company**, refer a member of the public to the broker's title company.

## D.  Quiet title action

1.  Used to clear title problems found in the abstract or title report.

2.  A quiet title action is a legal action.

# IV.  ESCROW OR CLOSING

## A.  Escrow/closing procedures

1.  Terms of escrow or closing are created by the purchase contract and finalized at closing.

## B.  Closing statement—debits and credits

1.  Credit to seller is anything that increases the amount of money the seller takes from the closing (**e.g., sales price**).

2.  Debit to seller is anything that decreases amount of money the seller takes from the closing (e.g., brokerage fee, mortgage payoff, or contract for deed).

3.  Credit to buyer is anything that decreases the amount of money the buyer must bring to closing (e.g., earnest money, **new loan**, or contract for deed). **Remember: All loans are always a buyer credit.**

4.  Debit to buyer is anything that increases the amount of money the buyer must bring to the closing (e.g., sales price, **recording the warranty deed, loan origination, or discount points if paid by buyer**).

a)  Proration based on a 365-day year or 360-day year (30-day months)—the exam will state which one to use. Rent is paid in advance, and mortgage interest is paid in arrears.

b)  Taxes can be in advance or in arrears.

c)  Rents are prorated.

d)  Security deposits transfer to the new owner and **ARE NOT prorated.**

## FIGURE 10.1

### How Paid Items are Recorded on the Settlement Worksheet and Closing Statement

| Selected Items | Details to Remember | Settlement Worksheet | Closing Statement |
|---|---|---|---|
| **Sales price** | | **Debit buyer, credit seller** | **Appears on both buyer's and seller's** |
| Earnest money | | Credit buyer, debit closer* | Appears on buyer's only |
| **Assumed loan amount** | **Principal remaining on loan assumed by buyer** | **Credit buyer, debit seller** | **Appears on both buyer's and seller's** |
| **Accrued interest on assumed loan** | **Prorated seller owes buyer for month of closing** | **Debit seller, credit buyer** | **Appears on both buyer's and seller's** |
| Seller carry loan amount | Reduces seller's cash at closing | Credit buyer, debit seller | Appears on both buyer's and seller's |
| Broker's commission | Negotiable Usually seller pays | If seller pays, debit seller, credit broker | If seller pays, appears on seller's only |
| **Owner's (buyer's) title insurance** | **Negotiable based on tradition** | **Debit seller, credit closer*** | **Appears on seller's only** |
| Mortgagee's (lender's) title insurance | Buyer pays lender's policy | Debit buyer, credit closer* | Appears on buyer's only |
| **Notary fee for warranty deed** | **Who signs document pays notary; seller signs deed** | **Debit seller, credit closer*** | **Appears on seller's only** |
| **Recording of warranty deed** | **Recording deed benefits buyer/grantee** | **Debit buyer, credit closer*** | **Appears on buyer's only** |
| Notary fee for deed of trust | Buyer signs promissory note and deed of trust at closing | Debit buyer, credit closer* | Appears on buyer's only |
| Tenant security deposits | Not prorated; belong to tenants | Debit seller, credit buyer | Appears on both buyer's and seller's |
| Rents | Prorated; paid in advance | Debit seller, credit buyer | Appears on both buyer's and seller's |
| **New loan amount** | **Figures from the new lender** | **Credit buyer, single entry** | **Appears on buyer's only** |
| **Net loan proceeds** | **New loan closing** | **Debit closer* only** | **Does not appear on either** |
| Taxes for the preceding year if unpaid | Credit depends on circumstances | Always debit seller, may credit buyer or closer* or new lender | Debit seller |
| Special taxes (special assessments) | May be paid off or assumed | If assumed, no entry; if paid, debit seller | Appears on seller's only |

Remember: All loans are always a buyer credit.

* The closer could be the broker or the escrow or closing company.

## V.    TAX ASPECTS

### A.    Capital gains

1.    Principal residence

    a)    There is no tax on the first $250,000 of gain (single) or $500,000 of gain (married) from the sale of a principal residence.

    b)    Owner must have lived in the residence **two out of the past five years** (does not have to be consecutive).

2.    Investment property—1031 tax-deferred exchange

    a)    Used by investment property owners to defer payment of capital gains taxes

    b)    Allows an investor to sell one property and buy another without paying capital gains tax

        (1)    The investor will not have to pay taxes at closing on the first property and can defer the taxes owed to the new property. The investor will not have to pay taxes until selling the second property.

        (2)    There are many rules for how the exchange must be carried out.

### B.    Deductible items

1.    **Mortgage interest, property taxes** (ad valorem taxes), discount points, and certain loan origination fees are deductible.

    a)    **Remember: POIT (poet) is deductible—points, origination, interest, and taxes.**

2.    **Not** deductible—principal, homeowners' insurance premiums, and HOA (homeowners' association) fees.

3.    To obtain a deduction the taxpayer must use an itemized return.

### C.    Depreciation tax deduction for investment property

1.    **Tax advantages such as <u>depreciation</u> often offset the disadvantage of liquidity.**

    a)    Depreciation is treated as an expense and is a line item on an income statement.

    b)    Depreciation can only be applied to the building and not the land, since land does not wear out over time.

2.    Residential income property must be depreciated over a 27½-year period using straight-line depreciation.

3.    Commercial income property must be depreciated over 39 years using straight-line depreciation.

4.  <u>Straight-line depreciation</u> requires that an asset must be depreciated by equal amounts each year over its useful life. (Variable, accrued, and passive depreciation are not used for this deduction.)

   a)  To determine how much an improvement has depreciated, divide the value by the number of years being depreciated, and multiply that by the number of years already taken.

      (1)  For example, a property with improvements that is valued at $390,000 and is being depreciated over 39 years will have depreciated by how much after 10 years?

      $390,000 \div 39 \times 10 = \$100,000$

# UNIT 11

# Real Estate Math Review

The national real estate licensing examination contains a relatively small number of calculations related to real estate transactions and decisions. Generally, these calculations are straightforward and easy. With a little work, you can be prepared to answer these exam questions correctly. The following review provides methods for performing the calculations and ways to remember how to manipulate the numbers.

Real estate students have widely different backgrounds and experience in handling these calculations. If you haven't done numeric calculations in quite some time, this unit will provide simple explanations and methods to guide you to the proper solutions for the problems you are most likely to face. If you are experienced in math, you will still need to understand how the world of real estate deals with many of these calculations.

## I. SIMPLE BASICS

### A. Using a calculator

1. You will have a simple calculator available during your examination, and you will not be allowed to bring in your own. The testing services provide calculators that include the ability to add, subtract, multiply, and divide. These calculators perform calculations in the standard way. For example, if you are adding the numbers 12, 15, and 37, you simply key in the problem as you would visualize it: 12 + 15 + 37.

   a) Key in the number 12 on the keypad (you should see the digits on the display).

   b) Press the + key.

   c) Key in the number 15 (only the new number will show in the display).

   d) Press the + again (the sum of the first two numbers will appear).

   e) Key in the next number, 37.

   f) Press the = key. Using the = key finishes the calculation and displays the solution (64).

2. There is usually a clear button that is often marked as CLR or C. Touching this button erases any numbers or actions that are in the calculator's memory. It is a good idea to press this key at the start of all calculations.

### B. Decimals and fractions

1. Decimals and fractions express parts of whole numbers, since not all calculations come out evenly. ½ is a fraction that expresses 1 part out of 2. It is really a division problem stated as 1 divided by 2. Calculators and computers are not set up to easily deal with fractions, so they are converted to decimal fractions by actually performing the calculation. On the calculator, 1 ÷ 2 = .5 or 0.5 (these are the same thing).

   a) For example, if you are calculating what part of the month of June 19 days represents, this would be 19 days (the part) divided by 30 days (the whole month). You could state it as

19/30, but that is probably not an available exam answer and would be difficult to use on a calculator. Instead complete the division indicated by the bar or slash mark: 19 ÷ 30 = 0.6333.

Depending on the calculator, this could look like 0.63333333 … (to the end of the display). This would occur on a floating decimal calculator. It could also look like 0.63 if the calculator is set to display only two decimal places. The calculator available for the exam will most likely have the floating decimal display.

2. If you are solving a multiple step problem that will use the first result in another step, leave the first calculated result on the display (don't touch CLR or C). If you instead write down the 0.63 display, clear the calculator, then key in just 0.63 you will only be using part of the actual calculated decimal fraction. Most of the time, you would not detect any difference in the final calculated result compared to the test answer choices, but if you are involved in a million dollar property sale, it could lead to a significant error for things like loan payments or tax prorations. These errors are called *rounding errors* because when you cut off the extra digits from the first calculation, you are rounding the number.

3. If you are using a floating decimal calculator, you can round a displayed result to match the exam answer choices—usually no more than four places to the right of the decimal point. For rounding, look one digit beyond the number of places in the exam answer (in the example above, the fifth digit beyond the decimal) and if the next digit is 5 or greater, increase the last digit in the rounded answer by 1. If the next digit is 4 or less, just cut off the digits beyond the fourth digit without adjusting the last digit.

   a) For example, if you are dividing $34 into 13 parts, you will get: 34 ÷ 13 = 2.61538462 …

      If the answer is to be in dollars and cents, you need to round to just two decimal places. Because the third digit is 5, you would round to $2.62 to match the correct exam choice.

4. If you are using a calculator that allows you to set the number of decimal places displayed, be sure to set it to display at least as many decimal places as the answers require. In the calculation above, if you had the display set to zero decimals, you would see a display of 3 which would likely be confusing, especially if an incorrect answer choice was $3 to test your understanding of rounding errors.

## C. Percentages

1. Percentages are another way to use decimals. Normal decimals represent parts of the whole number 1 (or 1.000000). In the first example, ½ = 0.5 or 0.50 (the same thing). Percentages relate the same part to the whole number 100. If the decimal fraction is 0.50, multiply that decimal by 100 and add a percent sign (%) to get the percentage: 0.50 × 100 = 50%.

   a) You can always change a decimal into a percentage by multiplying by 100. To convert a percentage to a decimal, divide by 100: 50% ÷ 100 = 0.50 as a pure decimal fraction.

   b) Note that you can make either conversion by simply moving the decimal point two places. To convert a percent to a decimal, move the decimal point two places to the left: 50% = 0.50. To convert a decimal to a percent, move the decimal point two places to the right: 0.25 = 25%.

2.  Some calculators have a % key to do this conversion. Be careful, they do not all work in the same way. Unless you are sure how the % key works on a particular calculator, just do the simple conversion yourself.

## II.   AREA CALCULATIONS

■  The area of a lot and the floor area of a structure are both common calculations in real estate. In practice, many of these can be quite complex and are the appropriate specialty of a land surveyor or possibly an appraiser.

### A.  Area of a lot

1.  For test purposes, most lots will be rectangles or squares. The lot is usually measured in feet which may be signified by the ' symbol (e.g., 25 feet may appear as 25').

2.  *Frontage* is a term used to describe the dimension of a lot that lies along a street (or sometimes along a lake or river) since this exposure may be very valuable for commercial exposure or access to recreational amenities. Traditionally, frontage is the first number used in describing the lot. A 65 foot by 110 foot lot has a frontage of 65 feet and is 110 feet deep, meaning the distance between the front lot line and the rear lot line.

3.  The area of a rectangle is calculated as: **Area = Width × Length**. If the lot dimensions are in feet, the result will be the area in square feet. A square foot is simply one foot wide and one foot long.

4.  Practice questions

    a)  What is the area of a lot 70 feet by 200 feet? (See Figure 11.1.)

        Area of a rectangle = Length multiplied by Width (A = L × W)

        A = _____ × 200' = _____ square feet

        The frontage (street front) is _____

    (1)  Solution: 70 × 200 = 14,000 square feet. The frontage is 70.

    b)  What would the above lot sell for at $3 per square foot plus a $5 premium per front foot?

    (1)  Solution: Area: A = 70' × 200' = 14,000 square feet. Selling price: 14,000 square feet × $3 per square foot = $42,000. Plus 70 front feet × $5 = $350 premium in addition to the price per foot. $42,000 + $350 = $42,350 selling price.

**FIGURE 11.1**

**Lot for Practice
Question a.**

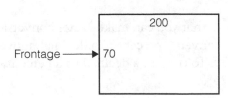

## B. Area of a building

1.  For most uses, the square footage or floor area of a building is measured using the exterior dimensions of the foundation. This sounds simple, but foundations may have many sides or even curved walls. In addition, some designs have upper levels that extend beyond the foundation. Different market areas have different traditions about which areas are included or excluded in square footage calculations, such as garages or basement areas. You will learn about these differences in the local practices of your community. For testing purposes, square footage problems are usually simple rectangles. To calculate the square footage or area of a two-story house, include the square footage of both levels.

2.  Practice questions

    a)  What is the square footage of a single-level house with exterior dimensions of 75 × 32 feet?

        (1)  Solution: A = 75' × 32' = 2,400 square feet

    b)  What would be the square footage of the same house if it had two stories?

        (1)  Solution: A = 75' × 32' × 2 (stories) = 4,800 square feet

    c)  A residential lot is 65' × 110' and zoning limits the home's footprint (which means the building cannot exceed these dimensions but can have more height) to 40% of the lot. What is the square footage of the largest two-story house that can be built on the lot?

        (1)  Solution: A = 65' × 110' = 7,150 square feet for the total lot. Allowed footprint = 7,150 × 0.4 = 2,860 square feet for the footprint; for two stories, 2,860 × 2 = 5,720 square feet.

## C. Price per square foot

1.  Appraisers often compare the price per square foot among properties they are evaluating, and in some markets, buyers are concerned with the price per square foot.

    a)  Price per square foot = Selling price ÷ Area in square feet

2.  Practice questions

    a)  What is the price per square foot of a house that measures 35' × 40' that recently sold for $220,000?

        (1)  Solution: A = 35' × 40' = 1,400 square feet. $220,000 ÷ 1,400 = $157.14 per square foot

    b)  If an industrial lot is 250' × 375' and sold for $1.15 per square foot, what was its sales price?

        This is best done as a chain calculation where instead of finding the area, writing it down, and then multiplying by the price per square foot, you key it into your calculator as: 250' × 375' × $1.15 = price. The chain calculation avoids possible rounding errors as mentioned above.

        (1)  Solution: Price = 250' × 375' × $1.15 = $107,812.50

**FIGURE   11.2**

**Circle Formulas**

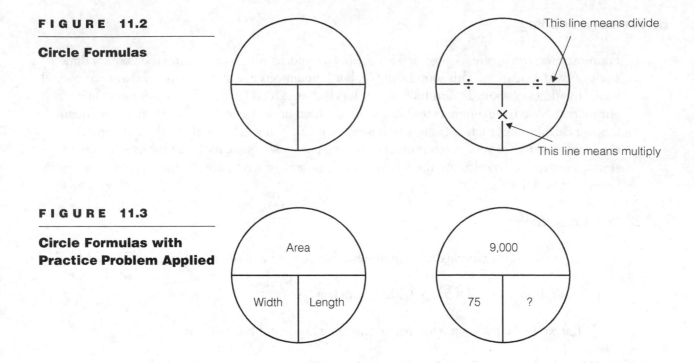

This line means divide

This line means multiply

**FIGURE   11.3**

**Circle Formulas with Practice Problem Applied**

## III.    INTRODUCTION TO CIRCLE FORMULAS

- Many real estate calculations involve three parts, and if you know two of them, you can calculate the third. For example, in area calculations there might be a question such as, if a lot has an area of 9,000 square feet and the frontage is 75 feet, how deep is the lot?

- Area = Width × Length, which means 9,000 = 75 × Length. What should you do next? Circle formulas are a simple tool for remembering what to do. You are not required to use them, but they can be very helpful. (*See* Figure 11.2)

- Figure 11.3 is what this problem would look like in a circle formula.

- The circle in Figure 11.3 shows what is needed: Length = Area ÷ Width = 9,000 ÷ 75.

- Solution: 9,000 ÷ 75 = 120 feet deep

### A.  Property Tax Calculations

1. Property taxes are charged (levied) based on an assessment rate. The assessor (usually a county official) uses mass appraisal methods to place a value on each privately-owned property in the jurisdiction, which is usually the county, township, or similar political division. The county commissioners or other similar body determines the total budget for the jurisdiction based on the services and needs of the county. The assessor then has the job of distributing the tax burden to each of the privately-owned properties. Most taxing areas have several classes of property such as residential, commercial, agricultural, and so on. These classes may have different taxing rates.

2. The assessor multiplies the actual value (as appraised by the assessor) by the tax rate for the class of property to determine the real property tax that the property owner will owe (*see* Figure 11.4).

   a)   Assessed value = Actual (appraised) value × Assessment rate

**FIGURE  11.4**

**Circle Formula for Taxes**

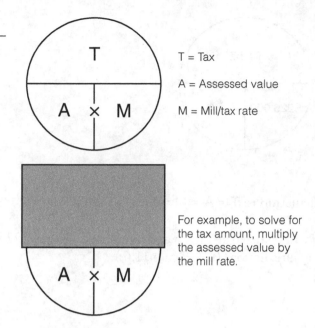

T = Tax

A = Assessed value

M = Mill/tax rate

For example, to solve for
the tax amount, multiply
the assessed value by
the mill rate.

3. The assessed value is smaller than the actual value.

   a)  Annual tax = Assessed value × Tax rate

4. The sum of all of the annual tax amounts must equal the total budget.

5. The tax rate is expressed as a fraction of the assessed value. It may be a percentage (an amount of tax per $100 of assessed value) or a mill which is an amount of tax per $1,000 of assessed value. This tax based on $1,000 of assessed value is called a mill rate. If the tax rate is given as a whole number such as 85 mills, convert it to a decimal fraction by dividing by 1,000 (85 ÷ 1,000 = 0.085). If the tax rate is dollars per $100 of assessed value, divide by 100.

6. Tax calculations based on the actual (appraised) value are often two-step calculations. The first step is to determine the assessed value needed for the circle formula.

   a)  If the assessor has determined that a property has an actual value of $350,000 and this class of property has an assessment rate of 29%, and the tax rate is 92 mills, what is the annual tax?

   Assessed value = Actual value × Assessment rate = 350,000 × 29% (remember 29% = 0.29) = $101,500. Use this value in the TAM circle formula (see Figure 11.5).

**FIGURE  11.5**

**TAM Circle Formula**

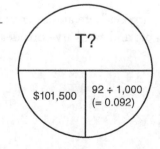

**FIGURE 11.6**

**Circle Formula for Practice Question b**

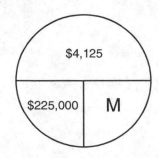

The final calculation is: T = A × M = $101,500 × 0.092 = $9,338.00 annual tax in dollars.

b) If a property will be taxed at $4,125 and its assessed value is $225,000, what is the mill rate for this taxing jurisdiction? (Use Figure 11.6.)

  (a) 0.02

  (b) 0.183

  (c) 0.0183

  (d) 183

(1) Solution: $4,125 ÷ $225,000 = 0.0183. Answer choice c is correct.

(2) The following explanations for each answer choice may explain why you answered the question differently:

  (a) You get this calculated result if you have a fixed decimal calculator showing only two decimal places. Change the decimal display to four places to see answer 3. Four places is safe for any exam calculation. A floating display will show more than enough decimal places.

  (b) Be sure to check decimal places and leading zeros.

  (c) This is the correct response.

  (d) If the question asked for the mills, not the mill rate, then the answer would have been 18.3 (multiply the calculated result by 1,000). It is very unlikely that a test question would mix mills and mill rate in one set of answers.

## IV. COMMISSIONS—GETTING PAID

■ Brokerage fees are generally paid based on a percentage of the selling price of a property. (*See* Figure 11.7)

■ Note: Commission rates are used for example purposes here and are not intended to imply any standard rate. Commission rates are always negotiable and can vary considerably with different types of property and geographic areas.

**FIGURE  11.7**

**Circle Formula for Commissions**

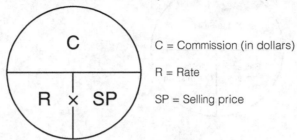

Hint: This circle formula is easy to remember: What you want to earn is CRiSP new dollars

C = Commission (in dollars)

R = Rate

SP = Selling price

To find the *commission* when the *rate* and *selling price* are known, cover up the C so R and SP are both below the line and separated by the ×. The formula is: C = R × SP

## A.  Example 1: Calculating a sales commission

1.  Croft agreed to pay a 6% commission on the home she listed with Broker Wright. The home sold for $80,000. How much was the commission?

    a)  R = Rate = 6% (0.06)
        SP = Selling price = $80,000
        C = R × SP
        C = 0.06 × $80,000 = _____

        (1)  Solution: 0.06 × $80,000 = $4,800

## B.  Example 2: Sales price

1.  The commission received was $4,800 and the rate was 6%. What was the sales price?

    a)  Commission divided by the rate: $4,800 ÷ 0.06 = _____

        (1)  Solution: $4,800 ÷ 0.06 = $80,000

    b)  To solve for the rate, divide the commission by the sales price: $4,800 ÷ $80,000 = 0.06 or 6 percent.

## C.  Net to seller

1.  To solve problems involving the net amount to the seller, a new circle formula (see Figure 11.8) and this calculation is needed: Sales price × (100% – Commission rate) = Net to seller.

2.  Sample problem

    a)  The seller will get 93% of the amount that the property sells for (100% of selling price minus the 7% commission) and the seller wants this net amount to be $80,000.

        Net to seller in this problem is $80,000.

        Sales price is the unknown value.

**FIGURE 11.8**

**Net to Seller Circle Formula**

(100% – Commission) is 93% which is how much of the sales price the seller will receive net of commission.

(1) Sales price = Net to seller ÷ 93% (this is 100% – Commission). To determine the sales price that will net the seller the amount wanted: $80,000 ÷ 0.93 = $86,021.51

3. On the test, you may be able to gain a lot of information from the answer choices. In the above problem, the listing price must be higher than the $80,000 the seller wishes to receive, so any answer choices smaller than $80,000 cannot be correct. Also, you could multiply each answer choice by 93% to see which one is closest to $80,000.

## D. Commission splits

1. Commissions are always negotiable between the broker (brokerage company) and the buyer or seller. Typically the managing broker delegates the power to negotiate this fee within limits to the salesperson or broker associate. The total commission is an agreed percentage of the selling price. The commission is then split between the brokerage and the salespeople or broker associates involved.

2. Companies will have a written agreement with each employed salesperson or broker associate for the way the fee will be split. For example, a company could keep 40% and give 60% to the salesperson who actually negotiated and serviced the listing. There may also be a split between the listing brokerage company and another brokerage firm that brought a buyer for the property. As an example, the listing brokerage might negotiate a 6% total commission to be paid by the seller. The listing company further agrees to split that fee with a cooperating brokerage that brings the buyer with 3% to each company. In that case, the commission is first divided between the companies, listing or selling/buyer side, and then split between each brokerage firm's salesperson or broker associate.

a) Example 1

For a property with a selling price of $200,000 with a 6% commission, the gross commission is $12,000. The listing company keeps $6,000 and shares the other $6,000 with the buyer's brokerage. The listing company then splits its portion of the fee, giving 60% to the listing associate ($3,600) and retains the rest ($2,400). If the listing company has a 50:50 split policy with its associates, both keep $3,000. (*See* Figure 11.9)

**FIGURE 11.9**

**Example 1: Commission Split**

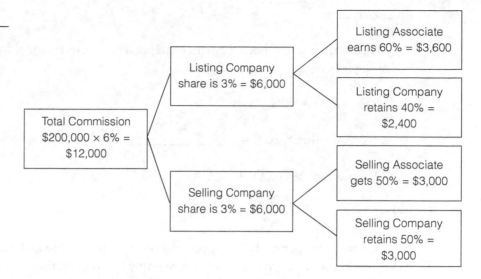

b)  Practice question 1

A seller lists his home with an agent, Sally, and negotiates a commission of 5.5%. The home is put on the market for $435,000. Another agent brings in an offer of $420,000, which is accepted. The two companies split the fee equally between them. Sally has an agreement to receive 60% of the company's commission on her listings. When the transaction closes, how much should Sally receive from her brokerage company?

(1)  Solution: $420,000 × 5.5% = $23,100. Split equally, each company receives $11,550. Sally's brokerage pays her 60%, which is $6,930.

c)  Practice question 2

A home sells for $150,000 at a commission rate of 6%. The listing brokerage has agreed to pay 55% of the commission to the selling brokerage. How much does the listing brokerage retain?

(1)  Solution: Listing brokerage pays out 55% and keeps 45% (calculate 100% − 55% = 45%). Selling price × 6% × 45% = $4,050.

## V.    LENDING AND MORTGAGE CALCULATIONS

■  Lenders use specific vocabulary to refer to the terms and conditions of various loan types. The following are a few common terms related to lending practices:

### A.  Loan-to-value ratio

1.  A ratio is a fraction relating the amount of a proposed loan to the value of the property. The ratio is usually stated as a percentage. For this purpose, lenders will use either the selling price of the property or the appraised value, **whichever is less**. Lenders offer their best terms to loans with a loan-to-value ratio of 80% or less. If the loan is 80% of the value, the down payment (20%) must make up the rest of the selling price.

2.  Loan-to-value ratio + Down payment percentage = 100%

3. Practice question

   a) What is the required down payment to get a new conventional loan with an 80% LTV ratio on a property appraised at $376,000?

   100% – 80% = 20% down

   $376,000 value × 20% = $_____

   (1) Solution: $376,000 × 20% = $75,200

## B. Equity

1. Lending practices permit home buyers to borrow considerable amounts of money for their purchase. As homeowners pay down the remaining balance on their home loan, they increase the part of the value of their home that is not pledged as security for a mortgage. This part is truly theirs.

   a) Equity is the current market value of the home minus all debts that use the home as security for a loan.

2. A property owned free and clear of all mortgages or home equity loans has 100% equity. For example, a home recently purchased using a 100% LTV loan guaranteed by the Veterans Administration has no equity.

3. Practice question

   a) A buyer purchased a property for $90,000 with 10% down. The current loan balance is $74,000. The property recently appraised for $116,000. What is the owner's equity?
      - (a) $16,000
      - (b) $42,000
      - (c) $116,000
      - (d) $83,000

   (1) Solution: Equity = Current value – Loans outstanding = $116,000 – $74,000 = $42,000. Answer choice b is correct.

## C. Discount points

1. Lenders may charge points to increase their yield (income) when making a loan. These points are calculated on the loan amount, not the total purchase price. Points could also be used to prepay some of the interest so the lender will reduce the interest rate on the loan without reducing the lender's income from the loan. One point is 1% of the loan amount.

2. Practice question

A lender is charging 2.5 points on an 80% LTV loan for a home purchased for $235,000. How much is the lender charging in dollars?

a) Step 1: Find the loan amount

Purchase price × LTV = Loan amount

b) Step 2: Calculate the dollar amount of the points

Loan amount × Points stated as a decimal fraction = Dollar amount

$235,000 × 80% × 2.5% = dollar amount = _____

(1) Solution: $235,000 × 80% × 2.5% = $4,700

## D. Buyer qualification

1. Lenders determine the maximum loan a buyer can afford using various percentages of the borrowers' monthly income before and after other debts, such as car loans and credit card debt. These percentages vary according to the type of loan and the amounts available for down payment. A test question might provide an income and a percentage to calculate the maximum loan payment. This payment refers only to the principal and interest at the current market interest rates.

2. Practice question

a) Jim and Jane are buying a house together, and they earn $65,000 per year combined. A lender states that they can qualify for payments up to 28% of their monthly income. What monthly payment could they qualify for?

Their combined income is $65,000 or $5,416.67 per month

28% × $5,416.67 = _____ per month principal and interest (P + I) payment

(1) Solution: 28% × $5,416.67 = $1,516.68

## E. Loan factors chart

1. Simple charts are available to estimate loan payments for fully amortized loans over various loan terms and at different interest rates. These charts show the dollars of payment per $1,000 for each combination of interest rates and loan terms. These payments represent the payment to principal and interest and do not take into account property taxes, insurance, homeowner fees, or any other ongoing property expenses (*see* Figure 11.10).

**FIGURE 11.10**

**Loan Factors per $1,000 for a Fully Amortized Loan**

| Interest | 15 years | 20 years | 25 years | 30 years |
|----------|----------|----------|----------|----------|
| 6.00% | 8.4386 | 7.1643 | 6.4430 | 5.9955 |
| 6.50% | 8.7111 | 7.4557 | 6.7521 | 6.3207 |
| 7.00% | 8.9883 | 7.7530 | 7.0678 | 6.6530 |
| 7.50% | 9.2701 | 8.0559 | 7.3899 | 6.9921 |

2. To use the chart, calculate how many thousands of dollars are in the loan (loan amount ÷ 1,000) and multiply by the factor for the loan interest rate and loan term.

3. Practice question

   a) A buyer is obtaining a $165,000 loan at 7%. If the buyer can afford a payment of $1,280 for principal and interest, what loan term will allow the buyer to pay off the loan in the shortest time period?

      (1) Solution: The loan will be 165 thousands. Using the 7% row, multiply the factor under each loan term by 165 to see if the payment is affordable: 15 years: 165 × 8.9883 = $1,483.07, which is too high so repeat until you calculate a payment of $1,280 or less. The answer is 20 years (165 × 7.7530 = $1,279.25).

### F. Loan payment chart

1. A loan payment chart is similar to a loan factors chart, but is calculated for a specific loan amount at a range of interest rates and loan terms. The dollar amounts in the chart are the actual payments. Each chart only relates to a specific loan amount that is given in the chart title (*see* Figure 11.11).

2. This type of chart can help match a loan qualification with the appropriate loan term and interest rate.

**FIGURE 11.11**

**Monthly Payments on a $165,000 Loan**

| Interest | 10 years | 15 years | 20 years | 30 years |
|----------|----------|----------|----------|----------|
| 5.00% | $1,750.08 | $1,304.81 | $1,088.93 | $885.76 |
| 5.25% | $1,770.31 | $1,326.40 | $1,111.84 | $911.14 |
| 5.50% | $1,790.68 | $1,348.19 | $1,135.01 | $936.85 |
| 5.75% | $1,811.19 | $1,370.18 | $1,158.44 | $962.90 |
| 6.00% | $1,831.84 | $1,392.36 | $1,182.11 | $989.26 |
| 6.25% | $1,852.62 | $1,414.75 | $1,206.03 | $1,015.93 |
| 6.50% | $1,873.54 | $1,437.33 | $1,230.20 | $1,042.91 |
| 6.75% | $1,894.60 | $1,460.10 | $1,254.60 | $1,070.19 |
| 7.00% | $1,915.79 | $1,483.07 | $1,279.24 | $1,097.75 |

3. Practice question

    a) A couple who earns $4,950 per month after taxes wants to make a mortgage payment of no more than 25% of their monthly earnings. Using Table 10.2, determine which interest rate and term will give the couple the payment closest to what they are seeking.

        (1) Calculate their maximum monthly payment: $4,950 × 25% = _____

        (2) Find the payment closest to their maximum payment without going over it. They can afford the loan at _____% for _____ years.

        (3) Solution: (1) $4,950 × 25% = $1,237.50; (2) A loan at 6.5% over 20 years has a payment of $1230.20 (the closest payment without going over).

## G. Interest calculations

1. Loan interest calculations involve the interest rate (usually stated as an annual percentage), the amount of the loan (the principal sum), and the dollars of interest. Some calculations are for annual interest and must be done with an annual rate to yield an annual interest amount. Other calculations are for monthly interest and must use a monthly rate to yield a monthly payment.

2. Real estate loans are generally paid 12 times a year on the same date each month. As a result, monthly payment calculations for the entire loan are based on 1/12 of the year and 1/12 of the annual interest rate. These calculations are not based on the number of days in a particular month. The lender simply computes the payments for 360 total payments for a 30-year loan and expects to receive 12 payments each year.

3. Most questions on the exam will require monthly interest so it is important to remember to divide the annual number by 12.

4. For interest calculations, use the circle formula in Figure 11.12 with the following:

I = Interest amount (annual number will need to be divided by 12 to get monthly amount)

R = Rate of interest

P = Principal sum (the amount borrowed)

**FIGURE 11.12**

**Circle Formula for Interest**

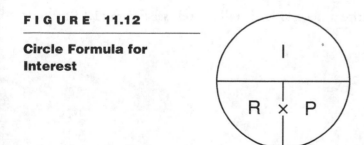

### H. Monthly loan payments

1. Most real estate loans first have payments that include amounts set aside to pay property taxes and hazard insurance. They are referred to as PITI payments, which stands for principal, interest, taxes, and insurance. The lender will collect the taxes and insurance payments in an impound or escrow account and will make the payments directly to the tax authority or insurance carrier at the appropriate time. Calculate these payments using the principal plus interest from a loan payment table or loan factor chart plus 1/12 of the annual taxes and 1/12 of the annual hazard insurance.

2. Practice question

   a) Mary and Fred are getting a new first loan to purchase a $250,000 house. They will put 20% down and are getting a 6.5% loan for 30 years. The property taxes will be $2,100 per year, and the insurance will be $915 per year. Using this information and Figure 11.10, calculate their monthly payment.

      (1) Solution:

      Loan factors: 6.5% for 30 years = 6.3207 × _____ = _____ P + I   $1,264.14

      Taxes: $2,100 ÷ 12 =                                    _____ T          175.00

      Insurance: $915 ÷ 12 =                                  _____ I          76.25

                                                  PITI = _____      $1,515.39

## VI.  PRORATION

**A. At settlement or closing, certain expenses must be equitably divided between the seller and buyer. For example, if the seller paid a bill in advance for water and sewer service, it is fair to calculate the cost of the buyer's part of the billing period and reimburse the seller at closing for that amount.**

**B. When taking the exam, the problem should be prorated as stated in the test question.**

**C. Points to consider**

1. On the national/general license exam, it will normally be identified who is responsible for the closing day.

2. The party who is identified as having the day of closing will owe or need to be paid for that full day.

3. It may help to draw a timeline for the entire water and sewer bill period (*see* Figure 11.13).

**FIGURE  11.13**

**Proration Diagrams**

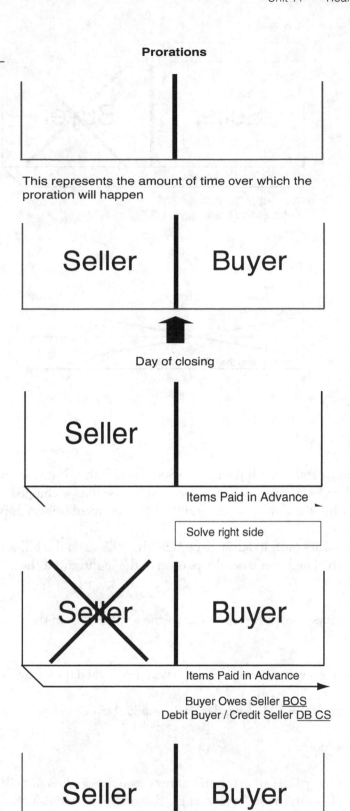

Prorations

This represents the amount of time over which the proration will happen

Seller | Buyer

Day of closing

Seller

Items Paid in Advance

Solve right side

Seller | Buyer

Items Paid in Advance

Buyer Owes Seller <u>BOS</u>
Debit Buyer / Credit Seller <u>DB CS</u>

Seller | Buyer

Items Paid in Arrears

**FIGURE 11.13**

**Proration Diagrams
(continued)**

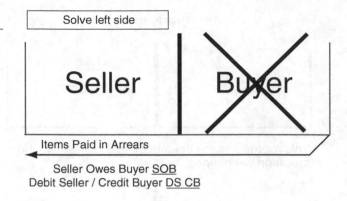

Items Paid in Arrears

Seller Owes Buyer <u>SOB</u>
Debit Seller / Credit Buyer <u>DS CB</u>

**FIGURE 11.14**

**Timeline for Practice
Question 1**

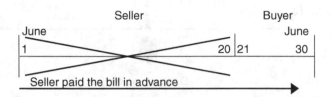

4. Practice question 1

A seller paid a $60 water bill for June in advance. If the closing is on June 20, how will the bill be divided between the seller and buyer and how will it be charged on the settlement statements if the seller has the day of closing and the bill is prorated using a 360-day year?

The buyer always owes in advance because the seller paid the bill on the first of June for the entire month. The buyer owes the portion of the month from the 21st through the 30th or 10 days to the seller.

To find the days the buyer owes, subtract the total days from the seller's last day: 30 − 20 = 10 days.

The formula is always the same: Total amount ÷ Total days × Days owed.

a) Solution: $60 ÷ 30 ($2 per day) × 10 = $20. Buyer owes seller: debit buyer and credit seller.

5. Practice question 2

a) A seller has paid quarterly homeowners' association dues of $101.20. If the closing is on August 17 with the seller having the day of closing and using a 360-day year, which would be the correct entry on the settlement statement?

   (a) $48.35 debit buyer

   (b) $101.20 credit seller

   (c) $52.85 debit buyer

   (d) $48.35 debit seller

(1) Solution: The timeline is July 1 through September 30. With 30 days in each month, the total days are 90. For a bill paid in advance, the buyer will always owe the seller (BOS), so calculate the buyer's part. The buyer's first day is August 18. Buyer's days = 30 – 17 in August = 13 + 30 for September = 43 days. Seller already paid, so buyer owes seller (debit buyer). 101.2 ÷ 90 = $1.12 per day × 43 days = $48.35. Answer choice a is correct.

6. Practice question 3

a) Taxes on a home will be paid in arrears on January 1 of next year. The taxes for the preceding year were $1,200. With a sale closing on April 15 with the buyer having the day of closing and using a 365-day year, how will taxes be handled at closing?

   (a) $858.08 debit buyer, $858.08 debit seller

   (b) $861.37 credit seller, $861.37 debit buyer

   (c) $338.63 credit seller, $338.63 credit buyer

   (d) $341.92 debit seller, $341.92 credit buyer

(1) Solution: For bills paid in arrears, the seller will always owe the buyer (SOB) because the buyer will pay the entire tax bill next year. The buyer is owed the seller's portion for the time the seller occupied the property. The seller's time is January 1 through April 15 (31 + 28 + 31 + 14 = 104 days). $1,200 ÷ 365 = $3.29 per day (leave answer in calculator to avoid rounding) × 104 days = $341.92. Seller owes this amount to the buyer who will pay the entire bill later. Debit the seller $341.92. Answer choice d is correct.

## VII.  APPRAISAL AND VALUATION

### A. Appreciation and depreciation

1. Practice question

a) A home is located in an area that has declined in value by 10% over the last 3 years. If the home was bought 3 years ago for $185,000, what would be its estimated current value based on this information?

   (a) $205,000

   (b) $166,500

   (c) $129,000

   (d) $179,600

**FIGURE  11.15**

**Circle Formula for Appreciation and Depreciation**

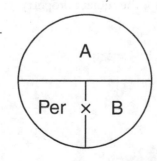

(1) Solution: Use the circle formula to solve the problem:

A (after) is needed

Per (for depreciation): 100% − Loss = 100% − 10% = 90%

B (before): $185,000

A = Per × B = 0.9 × $185,000 = $166,500 (Answer choice b is correct.)

## B. Tax depreciation

1. One income tax advantage of investment properties is that they may be depreciated during their lifetime to represent the wearing out of the asset. A non-residential commercial property may be depreciated over 39 years. The amount of the depreciation is calculated using a method called *straight line depreciation* in which the total value of the structure (not including land) is depreciated in 39 equal amounts over 39 years. This depreciation is purely an income tax calculation and is not directly related to the physical deterioration, functional obsolescence, or external obsolescence of the property.

2. Practice question

   a) An investor owns a commercial building valued at $390,000. Using straight line depreciation over 39 years, calculate the following:

      (1) How much does the building depreciate each year?

         (a) Solution: $390,000 ÷ 39 years = $10,000 per year

      (2) After 9 years, how much would the investor have taken in depreciation?

         (a) Solution: $10,000 × 9 = $90,000

## C. Competitive market analysis

1. Practice question

   a) A real estate sales associate is preparing a CMA for a potential listing. The listing property has 1,800 square feet, two bedrooms, one bath, and a fireplace. The home across the street sold for $181,000 and has 1,800 square feet, two bedrooms, two baths, and no fireplace. A home on the next street over sold for $175,000 and has 1,800 square feet, two bedrooms, one bath, and no fireplace. If an extra bath is worth $5,000 and a fireplace adds $3,000, what would be the estimated market value for the subject property?

      (a) $181,000
      (b) $179,000
      (c) $175,000
      (d) $185,000

(1) Solution:

| | Subject | Across street | | Next street | |
|---|---|---|---|---|---|
| Sold price | | | $181,000 | | $175,000 |
| Area | 1,800 | 1,800 | — | 1,800 | — |
| Bedrooms | 2 | 2 | — | 2 | — |
| Baths | 1 | 2 | −5,000 | 1 | — |
| Fireplace | 1 | 0 | +3,000 | 0 | +3,000 |
| Total adjustments | | | −2,000 | | +3,000 |
| Adjusted price | | | $179,000 | | $178,000 |

Estimated market value = $179,000 (do not average the two). Answer choice b is correct.

## D. Capitalization and cap rate

1. The income approach to value is used for many income-producing properties because the investor is interested in the income from the rents. Converting future net income to an estimate of value is called capitalization and is a primary tool for commercial property appraisers. A capitalization rate represents the yield or return on investment that an investor demands.

   a) Capitalization is the process of converting estimated future income into a value.

   b) Net operating income

      (1) The calculation of future income is based on a property's annual NOI

      | | |
      |---|---|
      | Potential annual gross income | $66,000 |
      | − Bad debt (2%) | − 1,320 |
      | − Vacancy (3%) | − 1,980 |
      | Effective gross income | $62,700 |
      | − Operating expenses | − 29,400 |
      | = NOI | $33,300 |

   c) Cash flow = I (net operating income) minus debt service

   d) Capitalization math

**FIGURE 11.16**

**Circle Formula for Capitalization**

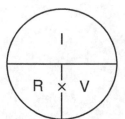

Income = Rate × Value
I = Net operating income
R = Capitalization rate (investor rate of return, also affected by market forces)
V = Value (what can be paid for a property to get the expected return)

Three relationships: I = R × V; R = I ÷ V; V = I ÷ R

2. Practice question

a)  A small office building has gross rental income of $60,000 per year. The owner pays an average of $18,000 per year in expenses. If an investor is seeking a capitalization rate of 7%, what would this property be worth?

   (a)  $857,143

   (b)  $420,000

   (c)  $7,000,000

   (d)  $600,000

   (1)  Solution: Income (NOI) = $60,000 – $18,000 = $42,000 annual net operating income. V = I ÷ R = $42,000 ÷ 0.07 = $600,000. Answer choice d is correct.

## E. Gross rent multiplier

1.  An investor considering buying a smaller residential property for rental use might use the gross rent multiplier (GRM) for a rough estimate of the property's value. The method does not take into account vacancies or expenses of a building.

2.  The gross rent multiplier is derived from information from several similar rental properties in the area using a circle formula such as Figure 11.17.

3.  GRM values from several properties are reconciled similar to comparables in an appraisal. The investor then applies the GRM with the formula V = Rent × GRM. A GRM number at or above 100 indicates a monthly multiplier while a smaller number, such as 12, would indicate an annual multiplier.

4.  When solving a GRM problem, it is important that the income and multiplier match (annual multiplier for annual income and monthly multiplier for monthly income).

**FIGURE 11.17**

**Circle Formula for Gross Rent Multiplier**

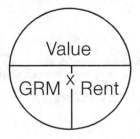

5. Practice question

    a)   If the multiplier in the neighborhood is 150 and a property has annual income of $12,000, what is its value?

        (a)  $150,000

        (b)  $175,000

        (c)  $102,000

        (d)  $196,000

    (1)  Solution: 150 (monthly multiplier—see #3 above) × (12,000 ÷ 12 = $1,000 per month) = $150,000. Answer choice a is correct.

# UNIT 12

# National Portion True/False Questions

The national portion of the Real Estate License Exam comprises 80 scored questions. These true/false questions are organized by the following topics.

General Principles of Agency   92

Contracts   98

Practice of Real Estate   104

Financing   108

Finance Math   117

Valuation and Market Analysis   119

Valuation Math   125

Property Ownership   127

Land-Use Controls and Regulations   135

Specialty Areas   139

Mandated Disclosures   140

Transfer of Title   142

# GENERAL PRINCIPLES OF AGENCY

(Test questions: Salesperson 10; Broker 11)

| | | |
|---|---|---|
| 1. | Listing Agent Anita, based on what the seller has told her, informs a buyer that damage has been fixed, when it is obvious it has just been painted over. Anita is guilty of puffing. | F misrepresentation |
| 2. | An agent can disobey a principal if a law would otherwise be broken. | T |
| 3. | Under no circumstances can an agent disobey a principal, since the agent owes the principal obedience. | F An agent must disobey if obeying would break the law. |
| 4. | Agents owe fiduciary duties to the person who pays them. | F to the person who employs them |
| 5. | Agents owe fiduciary duties to their principal. | T |
| 6. | Agents owe fiduciary duties to their customers. | F owe honesty and fair dealing |
| 7. | Agent Carl, representing Seller Kathy, receives an offer. Carl does NOT believe Buyer Janice can afford the property. He should reject the offer. | F Agent Carl must present all offers but should advise seller of his concerns. |
| 8. | A broker informs a salesperson that a client of the firm confidentially told the broker that he would accept less than the asking price. The salesperson should inform potential buyers of this fact. | F would violate fiduciary duty of confidentiality |
| 9. | The person who engages another to act for him under a contractual agreement is referred to as an agent. | F principal |
| 10. | Responsibilities of an agent to the principal include informing the principal of the amount and form of deposits for offers presented. | T |
| 11. | The obligation of an agent to represent a principal is created by a fiduciary agreement. | T |
| 12. | A fiduciary relationship exists between an agent and a principal. | T |
| 13. | If a licensed broker has found a buyer who is ready, willing, and able to buy under the terms of the listing and a contract to purchase has been signed by both parties, the broker has closed the sale. | F earned a commission |
| 14. | The law of agency applies to any relationship with a principal. | T |
| 15. | An agency relationship exists between the seller and the buyer. | F between the principal and agent |
| 16. | The term *agent* means "one who is granted authority to act on another's behalf." | T |

## QST A salesperson/broker associate could give legal advice:

| | | |
|---|---|---|
| 17. | When a buyer and seller disagree over a contract provision regarding forfeiture of earnest money | F |
| 18. | When the seller asks the salesperson to explain the legal protection afforded by a contract for deed | F |
| 19. | At the time of settlement | F |
| 20. | With the consent of her employing broker | F |
| 21. | After bringing the buyer and the seller together in a contract | F |
| 22. | If an engaged couple wishes to know how to take title | F A real estate professional should never give legal advice. |

| | | |
|---|---|---|
| 23. | A fiduciary relationship is commonly created by using an exclusive-right-to-sell agency listing. | T |
| 24. | A seller tells her listing broker that her house is structurally sound. The broker later discovers water damage in the basement. The broker is obligated to protect the seller and remain silent. | F must inform of damage |

**QST Under the law of agency, the broker representing a seller should:**

| | | |
|---|---|---|
| 25. | Present all offers to the principal | T |
| 26. | Disclose to buyers that the seller will accept less than the listed price | F |
| 27. | Account for all trust funds placed in the broker's control | T |
| 28. | Exercise care, obedience, loyalty, and accounting | T |
| 29. | Perform in the best interests of the broker | F principal |
| 30. | The commission received by a listing broker is set by the local board of REALTORS®. | F negotiation |
| 31. | Acting as an agent, a real estate broker may sign a purchase agreement on behalf of the principal. | F Special agents may not bind a principal. |
| 32. | When showing an office building to a prospective purchaser, the salesperson for the seller advises the buyer that the property will be very profitable in the future because of its location near a proposed light rail station. The salesperson's behavior might be an example of puffing. | F misrepresentation |
| 33. | When representing a family member, a licensee must *NOT* disclose this relationship to other parties to the transaction. | F Must disclose this material fact that could affect bargaining position. |
| 34. | Broker Ken has listed a home. He has fiduciary duties to unrepresented buyers. | F honesty, fair dealing, and care, but not fiduciary duties |
| 35. | In an open listing, the agency authority of all brokers is terminated when the house is sold by any broker or the owner. | T |
| 36. | A listing contract would be terminated by the death of the listing salesperson. | F The company owns the listing and will appoint someone else to help the seller. |
| 37. | The maximum commission rate that a broker may charge on the sale of improved property is a rate determined by the multiple listing services. | F Commissions are always negotiable. |
| 38. | Under an exclusive-agency listing, the broker is entitled to receive a commission, regardless of who sells the property. | F no commission if owner sells |
| 39. | A broker receives two offers within one hour for a property listed with him. The broker should submit to the seller the highest offer only. | F both offers at the same time |
| 40. | To receive a commission on an open listing, the broker will need to be the procuring cause of the sale. | T |

41. The law requires brokers to accept all listings that have been offered to them, as all sellers deserve representation.

F broker's choice

42. An exclusive-right-to-sell listing entitles the broker to a commission if the owner sells the property within the time period of the listing contract.

T

43. Under an exclusive-agency listing, if a buyer found a property on her own, the broker would still be entitled to be paid.

F In exclusive agency, brokers are not paid unless they or another broker find the property.

44. If a licensee acting solely as a seller's agent obeyed the seller's instructions to leave all discussions of property condition to the seller, a buyer could hold the agent liable for claims of misrepresentation.

T

45. A seller tells the broker that if the broker sells the property, the seller will pay them a commission. This is MOST likely an exclusive-agency listing.

F open listing

46. The principal owes the fiduciary duties of OLDCAR to the agent.

F Agent owes to principal.

47. An owner lists her home for $100,000, and the listing broker tells the prospective buyer to submit a low offer because the seller is desperate. The buyer offers $95,000, and the seller accepts. In this situation, the broker was unethical, but because no one was hurt, the broker's conduct is not improper.

F The broker violated the agency relationship by disclosing confidential information and was unethical.

48. A salesperson can advertise a listed property without identifying her employing broker.

F Broker's name must appear in the advertisement.

49. A doctor listed his home with a brokerage firm under an exclusive-right-to-sell agreement. In this situation, if the doctor dies, the listing contract will be terminated.

T

50. A real estate broker is usually a special agent.

T

51. All of a salesperson's licensed activities must be carried out in the name of his broker.

T

52. You are a broker who has listed a home for a neighbor. That means that you are a dual agent of the seller.

F You are the agent of the seller.

53. A man who owned a single-family house had his unlicensed son-in-law do the electrical work in preparing the home for sale. The man did not disclose this to the broker at the time of executing the listing or in the seller's property disclosure. After completion of the sale, the new owner suffered a financial loss because of the faulty electrical wiring done by the owner's son-in-law. The broker is innocent of any wrongful act.

T Brokers are not responsible for latent material facts.

54. The responsibilities of a broker in an agency relationship include accepting an offer for the seller.

F Offers may be accepted or rejected by the seller.

55. The listing broker owes fiduciary duty to the buyer.

F seller

56. A broker lists an accountant's property. The broker may bind the seller to a purchase contract.

F As special agent, broker may not bind the seller.

| | | |
|---|---|---|
| 57. | A salesperson sells a property listed by a different broker. The salesperson may accept her share of the commission from the other broker. | F She can only accept commissions from her own broker. |
| 58. | If a broker who represents a prospective buyer suggests offering less than the listing price, it is considered a violation of the broker's fiduciary relationship with the seller. | F Broker's fiduciary relationship is with the buyer. |
| 59. | A fiduciary must conform to the principal's legal instructions and owes loyalty to the principal. | T |
| 60. | A salesperson may receive a commission directly from a seller. | F commissions from salesperson's broker only |
| 61. | Listing agreements should be implied agreements. | F express, written agreements |
| 62. | A broker, representing a seller as an agent, is responsible for explaining the advantages and disadvantages of the offer to the seller. | T |
| 63. | A broker listed a home under an exclusive-right-to-sell listing contract. The seller generally is required to accept any offer at the listed price and terms. | F Listing is an employment contract with the broker. |
| 64. | A purchase contract has been terminated under the loan contingency. In this case, the broker will receive a commission. | F will not receive a commission since the property did not close |
| 65. | Listings may have an automatic renewal to extend the termination. | F must have a specific termination date with no automatic renewal |
| 66. | A seller's property disclosure is filled out by the broker and signed by the seller. | F completed and signed by the seller only |

**QST   Which of the following is *TRUE* of an open listing?**

| | | |
|---|---|---|
| 67. | The seller may employ any number of brokers. | T |
| 68. | Only one broker may act as an agent for the seller. | F |
| 69. | The broker is entitled to a commission upon procuring a buyer for the house for the seller. | T |
| 70. | The broker's commission is based on the excess over the sales price stated in the listing. | F |

**QST   Which of the following would legally terminate a listing with a broker?**

| | | |
|---|---|---|
| 71. | Bankruptcy of the brokerage firm | T |
| 72. | Death of the seller | T |
| 73. | An economic depression | F |
| 74. | Inability of the broker to find a buyer within the agreed time | T |
| 75. | Death of the salesperson | F contract is not with the salesperson |
| 76. | Salesperson moves to a new office with another broker. | F contract belongs to original broker |
| 77. | A broker should tell a customer not to share confidential information. | T |

| | |
|---|---|
| 78. A broker who states, "This is the best home in the city," is MOST likely puffing. | T |
| 79. All contracts belong to the brokerage firm, NOT the salesperson or broker associate. | T |
| 80. A salesperson/broker associate would NOT be responsible for finding latent material facts. | T Latent means hidden. |
| 81. A dual agent must have written consent of both parties she represents. | T |
| 82. A salesperson/broker associate can accept payment from buyers. | F only from the employing broker |
| 83. An express, written listing is preferred as it will give full protection to the brokerage and seller. | T |
| 84. Employing brokers are allowed to discuss commissions at REALTOR® meetings. | F Real estate professionals may not discuss commissions outside the office. |
| 85. A brokerage that takes an exclusive-agency listing would be less motivated to fully market the property due to competition with the seller. | T |
| 86. The listing broker who failed to follow the seller's directions for setting showings would be liable for any injuries caused to the buyer. | T |
| 87. Death of the salesperson/broker associate will terminate a listing. | F death of the employing broker or seller |
| 88. The protection or extension clause protects the broker after the termination of the listing. | T |
| 89. A broker who inflates a sales price in order to get a listing is acting unethically. | T |
| 90. It is acceptable to tell the seller you can get more money for her home than your CMA states, if you are competing against other brokers for the listing. | F unethical |

QST   An owner has given an exclusive-right-to-sell listing to a broker for a 6-month period. During the exclusive period, the owner also gives an open listing to another broker who produces a buyer. What is the owner's liability for payment of commission?

| | |
|---|---|
| 91. Only one commission must be paid, which both brokers share on a 50-50 basis. | F There is no agreement to split the commission. |
| 92. The owner is liable only to the first broker for the payment of a commission. | F The owner has agreed to pay both brokers. |
| 93. The owner is liable for payment of a commission to both brokers. | T |
| 94. The owner is liable only to the second broker for the payment of a commission. | F The exclusive-right-to-sell agreement states the broker will be paid regardless of who sells the property. |

| 95. | A broker states she will hold an open house every weekend. The broker holds only one open house in the first month but receives an offer at the end of the month, which the seller accepts. The seller may discount the broker's commission because the broker did not fully market the property. | F The seller's accepting the offer means the broker has done her job and should receive the full commission at closing. |
|---|---|---|
| 96. | A real estate professional is obligated to disclose any brokerage relationships prior to receiving confidential information. | T |
| 97. | A seller completes the seller's property disclosure to the *BEST* of his current actual knowledge. | T |
| 98. | Commissions are negotiable in every case. | T |
| 99. | Brokers are obligated to see that all parties are in compliance with lead-based paint disclosure. | T |
| 100. | A buyer may sign a representation agreement that makes the buyer responsible for payment of the broker's commission. | T |
| 101. | A salesperson leaving a company will always be allowed to take her listings. | F Contracts belong to the brokerage. |
| 102. | The listing agreement is considered to be terminated once the seller accepts an offer. | F on the specific termination date |
| 103. | The principal is the one who pays the broker. | F employs |
| 104. | A broker who states that all the students in the local school get high grades and go on to college is clearly puffing. | F misrepresentation |
| 105. | A broker who states the views of the mountains from a home are the best in the state is puffing. | T |
| 106. | A salesperson may accept the direct payment of referral fees from an out-of-state broker. | F Salespeople may only receive payments from the broker. |
| 107. | A salesperson is responsible for all earnest money and personal property given to them by a principal. | T |
| 108. | A buyer could use an exclusive agency contract to hire a broker. | T |
| 109. | Property managers are considered special agents. | F general agents |
| 110. | Common laws of agency are used if there is no applicable state law. | T |
| 111. | A buyer's broker has just discovered a material fact about a property that is under contract. The first person the buyer's broker should disclose the information to is the listing broker. | F the buyer who they represent, then the other parties |
| 112. | A listing would terminate upon expiration date or closing, whichever is first. | F Closing terminates the listing and a purchase contract obligates the broker to close the property. |
| 113. | A broker is allowed to pay a referral fee to an unlicensed member of the public if the individual gave a lead that created a sale. | F May not give referral fees to unlicensed individuals |
| 114. | Referral fees between brokers in different states are a common and acceptable practice. | T |

# CONTRACTS

(Test questions: Salesperson 11; Broker 12)

| | | |
|---|---|---|
| 1. | An example of a novation is a new contract replacing an old one. | T |
| 2. | A contract can be discharged when it cannot be legally accomplished based on impossibility of performance. | T |
| 3. | An executory contract is one that has been fully performed. | F  one yet to be performed |
| 4. | Earnest money is part of consideration and must be included in every contract. | F  Earnest money is not consideration and is not required. It is tied to liquidated damages in case of default. |
| 5. | A purchase agreement is binding on the buyer as soon as she makes the offer. | F  when acceptance is communicated |
| 6. | A purchase agreement is binding on the buyer upon the seller's acceptance. | F  binding when acceptance is communicated |
| 7. | In order for a contract for the sale of real property to be enforceable under the statute of frauds, the contract must be put in writing and signed by both parties. | T |
| 8. | A signed contract of sale legally binds each party to its terms and can be modified only by amendment. | T |
| 9. | A salesperson with full knowledge writes deceptive information in a sales contract. One of the parties to the contract acts on the information provided and incurs damages. Under these circumstances, the action of the salesperson constitutes duress. | F  fraud |
| 10. | A written lease for a term of 3 years is enforceable under the statute of frauds. | T |
| 11. | A contract that binds one party while allowing the other party to withdraw if certain conditions are NOT met is void. | F  voidable |
| 12. | A contract that has yet to be performed is an executory contract. | T |
| 13. | A signed contract of sale transfers legal title. | F  Deeds transfer title. |
| 14. | An agreement of sale put into writing is enforceable under the statute of frauds. | T |
| 15. | If a buyer and seller agree to a contract modification, they should sign an amendment. | T |
| 16. | A contract with a minor is voidable by either party to the contract. | F  only by the minor |
| 17. | If a seller misrepresents a material fact about the property, from the buyer's point of view the contract is unenforceable. | T |
| 18. | If one party to a contract takes legal action to force the other party to perform, it is called a suit for liquidated damages. | F  specific performance |
| 19. | In order to be valid, a purchase agreement must include a clause specifying the listing commission. | F  Commissions are not a part of a purchase agreement. |
| 20. | To be valid, a lease must contain a renewal option. | F  often ends on the termination date |

| | | |
|---|---|---|
| 21. | A buyer offers to purchase and signs a contract. The buyer later decides not to purchase and the seller has no recourse. This is MOST likely an option contract. | T |
| 22. | Earnest money is a deposit on a contract paid by the purchaser to the seller or the seller's broker. | T |
| 23. | Normally, if a lessor dies, the lease is terminated. | F  Leases do not normally terminate upon death. |
| 24. | In a sale-leaseback, the grantor becomes the lessor, and the grantee becomes the lessee. | F  Grantor is lessee, and grantee is lessor. |
| 25. | When an individual buys the right to purchase land in the future for a fixed price, the document used is a purchase agreement. | F  option |
| 26. | When a person leases land on which he or she has agreed to construct an office building, the lease is termed a ground lease. | T |
| 27. | Most real estate contracts are implied. | F  Real estate contracts should be express, written documents. |
| 28. | Contracts that have competent parties are MOST likely void. | F  valid |
| 29. | An option is generally defined as an informal agreement between a prospective purchaser and a listing broker that the purchaser can buy the listed property at a price quoted by the broker. | F  written contract between optionor and optionee |
| 30. | When a purchase agreement has been signed by all parties, the buyer is said to be the equitable owner or to have equitable title. | T |
| 31. | In order to be valid, a purchase agreement must include earnest money as consideration. | F  Earnest money is not consideration and is not required. |
| 32. | Earnest money is the money financed by the lending institution. | F  Earnest money is a good-faith deposit. |
| 33. | An executed contract has been completed. | T |
| 34. | A contract for sale conveys title to a property at the time it is signed by both parties. | F  binds parties to complete the sale |
| 35. | A purchase agreement binds the buyer and seller to complete the sale within a given period of time. | T |
| 36. | A novation is a new contract. | T |
| 37. | In a purchase agreement, the buyer has legal title and the seller has equitable title. | F  Seller has legal title, and buyer has equitable title. |
| 38. | If a contract includes a clause stating "time is of the essence," the parties to the contract are required to perform within a time limit established by the terms of the contract. | T |
| 39. | If a broker receives a counteroffer from a seller and presents it to the prospective buyer, the broker may show the property to other prospective buyers while waiting for the prospective buyer's response. | T |
| 40. | A counteroffer terminates the purchase agreement. | T |
| 41. | A bilateral contract is one in which only one party is legally bound to perform. | F  both parties |
| 42. | In order for a sales contract to be legally valid, it must contain a metes-and-bounds description. | F  any form of legal description |

| | | |
|---|---|---|
| 43. | To be enforceable, a contract to purchase must include the signature of the seller(s). | T |
| 44. | The statute of limitations requires that a real estate sales contract be in writing. | F statute of frauds |
| 45. | An oral real estate sales contract is not enforceable in a court action. | T |
| 46. | A void contract is one that binds one party but allows the other party to withdraw. | F voidable |
| 47. | In a purchase agreement, the name of the clause that states that the buyer will not be responsible to complete the purchase if the buyer cannot obtain financing is the acceleration clause. | F contingency clause |
| 48. | Rescission of a contract means that all parties are returned to the condition they held before the contract was executed. | T |
| 49. | A buyer and seller have entered into a valid purchase agreement. Prior to closing, the seller is killed in a plane crash. The contract is void. | F valid |
| 50. | Addenda add items to an offer. | T |
| 51. | If an option is not exercised, the optionor retains the option consideration. | T |
| 52. | Dan told Marie that he would pay her if she decided to sell the house. This is a bilateral contract. | F unilateral, as only Dan is obligated |
| 53. | An optionee is required to purchase the property. | F Optionee has the right to purchase. |
| 54. | The buyer has received a counter and decides to buy a different property. The buyer has no obligation to respond to the first seller. | T |
| 55. | The primary purpose of an option contract is to keep a property off the market for a certain period of time. | T |
| 56. | An option, when exercised, becomes a bilateral contract. | T |
| 57. | An offeror can withdraw an offer at any time prior to communication of acceptance. | T |
| 58. | A contract in which the intentions of the parties are shown by their actions is an express contract. | F implied contract |
| 59. | A lease that is signed by a person who is 17 years of age is void. | F voidable |
| 60. | A broker lists a home for $80,000. The broker brings an offer to the seller for $78,000, which is rejected by the seller. The broker obtains another offer of $80,000 for the seller. Before he can deliver the offer, however, the offeror withdraws it by calling the broker at the seller's home. There is an implied contract. | F no contract |
| 61. | An option is an example of a unilateral contract. | T |
| 62. | A contract that has no legal effect because it does NOT contain all essential requirements of a contract is void. | T |
| 63. | An office tenant has signed a lease that contains a hold harmless clause. During regular business hours, a visitor to the office is hit on the head by a falling shelf. The landlord is fully liable. | F The hold-harmless clause protects the landlord. |

| | | |
|---|---|---|
| **64.** | A lease transfers possession of real estate but *NOT* legal title at the time of signing. | T |
| **65.** | A tenant who pays a base rent and a percentage of the expenses has a percentage lease. | F  net lease |
| **66.** | A tenant who is renting a commercial property pays a certain percentage of the gross sales profit of the business in addition to the base rent. This is an example of a percentage lease. | T |
| **67.** | A tenant who has rented a residential property for a long period of time agrees to pay a slightly higher rent each year of her lease. This is an example of a ground lease. | F  graduated/step-up |
| **68.** | A tenant who is renting a residential property is allowed to apply rental payments to the purchase of the property. This is an example of a sale-leaseback. | F  rent with option to buy |
| **69.** | A gross lease is one whereby the landlord pays all property charges and the tenant pays a fixed monthly rent. | T |
| **70.** | A lease must be in writing to be enforceable, unless it is for a time period of 1 year or less. | T |
| **71.** | If the lessor sells the property to someone other than the lessee, the lease would be terminated. | F  The lease stays in force. |
| **72.** | When a leased property is sold, the seller must transfer all security deposits to the buyer. | T |
| **73.** | A tenant who has cause to use constructive eviction may give the landlord notice that she is not paying rent but will stay in the property until the complaints are resolved. | F  Tenants using constructive eviction must move out. |
| **74.** | In accounting for expenditures made on behalf of the principal, a manager of an apartment complex should consider maintenance, personnel salaries, and real estate taxes as operating expenses. | T |
| **75.** | A landlord gave a tenant a 2-year lease. The landlord died at the end of the first year, and the property was sold. The tenant must vacate the property. | F  The tenant's rights are not terminated by the death or sale and continue until the end of the lease term. |
| **76.** | Under conditions of climbing inflation, a property manager would be reluctant to negotiate a fixed lease. | T |
| **77.** | A buyer has contracted with a seller to purchase property. The closing was completed on March 31. The status of the contract on April 1 is executed. | T |
| **78.** | Minors always make contracts void. | F  voidable |
| **79.** | The default remedy available to both parties in the purchase agreement is liquidated damages. | F  specific performance |
| **80.** | Duress, fraud, minors, and misrepresentation make contracts voidable. | T |

**QST   The following are essential elements of all contracts:**

| # | Question | Answer |
|---|----------|--------|
| 81. | Competent grantor | F competent parties |
| 82. | Lawful purpose/objective | T |
| 83. | Consideration | T |
| 84. | Earnest money | F tied to default |
| 85. | In writing | T |
| 86. | Legal description | F required for a deed |
| 87. | Mutual agreement | T |
| 88. | A minor signing a contract typically makes it void. | F voidable |
| 89. | When one party to a contract sues the other, the suing party is seeking liquidated damages. | F specific performance |
| 90. | The buyer is in default, and the seller kept the earnest money. The contract included specific performance. | F liquidated damages |
| 91. | The buyer has used a contingency to terminate the contract, so in this case, the seller and listing broker will keep the earnest money. | F Must return it immediately. |
| 92. | The *BEST* contracts are express, written documents. | T |
| 93. | In the executory phase of a purchase contract, the buyer is the equitable owner. | T |
| 94. | Purchase agreements and leases are examples of unilateral contracts. | F bilateral |
| 95. | A contract that lacks a meeting of the minds is voidable. | F void because it lacks an essential element |
| 96. | Contingency clauses allow the holder to terminate a contract. | T |
| 97. | Constructive eviction is used by landlords if a tenant is in default. | F actual eviction |
| 98. | Mutual rescission would most likely occur when a buyer finds a better home to buy. | F only if there is a valid reason to break the contract |
| 99. | A seller who has offered one buyer a counterproposal must wait until the buyer accepts or rejects the offer before accepting another offer. | F Seller can withdraw the counteroffer at any time prior to communication of acceptance. |
| 100. | Competent parties means everyone is sane and sober. | T must also be over age 18 |
| 101. | If all essential elements are met, the contract is considered voidable. | F valid |
| 102. | A contract for the transfer of real estate that is *NOT* in writing is voidable. | F void |
| 103. | Lawful purpose or objective means all parties are of legal age. | F the purpose of the contract is legal |
| 104. | Consideration in a contract means the promises. | T |
| 105. | A buyer who terminates per the finance contingency has made the contract void. | F the valid contract has terminated |
| 106. | A buyer who terminates per a contingency will forfeit the earnest money. | F will have earnest money returned |
| 107. | The seller has decided not to sell the property that is under contract. The buyer's only recourse is liquidated damages. | F specific performance, sue to perform |

108. Earnest money is typically returned to the buyer if the buyer terminates under any contingency in the contract. | T

109. Meeting of the minds means all parties are in agreement and are ready to proceed with a contract. | T

110. A contract signed under duress or misrepresentation is void. | F  voidable

111. Salespeople should know the essential elements of contracts in order to determine what makes contracts valid, void, and voidable. | T

112. Competent grantor, meeting of the minds, lawful objective, consideration, and the document in writing all make a contract valid. | F  The parties need to be competent. Grantor is used with a deed.

113. Contracts should be expressed written agreements. | T

114. Implied contracts for the transfer of real estate are *NOT* enforceable per the statute of limitations. | F  statute of frauds

115. A counteroffer is a rejection of the original offer. | T

116. The seller agrees to sell for a set time and price in an option contract. | T

# PRACTICE OF REAL ESTATE

(Test questions: Salesperson 12; Broker 12)

| | | |
|---|---|---|
| **1.** | Someone who has recovered from a mental disability is protected under the Fair Housing Act. | T Mental disability, or a history of having had such a disability, is covered. |
| **2.** | A person who suffered from a mental disability but has now recovered is no longer protected under the Fair Housing Act or the Americans with Disabilities Act. | F History of having had such a disability is covered. |
| **3.** | A landlord may charge a handicapped tenant additional monies to pay for extra insurance. | F |
| **4.** | A landlord may require a handicapped tenant to restore his apartment to its original condition at termination of the lease. | T |
| **5.** | It is acceptable to discriminate on the basis of race in the rental of a duplex where the owner occupies the other unit. | F no exceptions for race |
| **6.** | An aggrieved party can file a federal lawsuit under the Fair Housing Act for up to 1 year following the alleged offense. | F 2 years to court; 1 year to make complaint to HUD |
| **7.** | A person who has been discriminated against can file a civil lawsuit in federal court for up to 2 years after the act has been committed. | T |
| **8.** | A property manager can market rental units as being for seniors only if 70% of the residents are at *LEAST* 65 years old. | F if 80% of residents are at least 55 years old |
| **9.** | Panic peddling, blockbusting, steering, and redlining are violations of the federal Fair Housing Act. | T |
| **10.** | Under the federal Fair Housing Act, it is illegal to discriminate on the basis of age. | F Age is not a protected housing class. |
| **11.** | A broker fails to show rental properties to minority prospects because the owners have indicated that they do not want to rent to minority tenants. This is a violation of the federal Fair Housing Act. | T |
| **12.** | A broker obtains listings in an integrated neighborhood by telling property owners that the value of their property is declining due to the influx of minority property owners. This is a violation of the federal Fair Housing Act. | T called blockbusting or panic selling |

**QST   The following actions are <u>in violation</u> of the federal Fair Housing Act:**

| | | |
|---|---|---|
| **13.** | Denying a renter a based on marital status | F not covered in federal law |
| **14.** | Denying housing to children in a building where 80% of the units have at *LEAST* one person over 55 living in them | F are exempt from familial status as long as 80% of the units have persons over age 55 |
| **15.** | Mr. Kerber lives in his house, rents out four extra rooms, and refuses to rent to students. | F Students are not a protected class. |
| **16.** | The landlord runs an ad for a studio apartment that states no children are allowed. | T |

17. National origin is the only protected classification contained in both the 1866 Civil Rights Act and the 1968 Fair Housing Act.

F race

18. The Equal Credit Opportunity Act (ECOA) prohibits discrimination based on a borrower's age.

T

19. It is acceptable to limit occupancy of studio apartments to adults only.

F Familial status states must allow children.

20. *Familial status* refers to whether the parties in question are married or single.

F children under age 18 or a pregnant woman

21. According to the federal Fair Housing Act, a handicapped individual is one with a physical or mental impairment that substantially limits one or more major life activities.

T

22. A person who is suffering from drug abuse is protected under anti-discrimination law.

F Drug abuse is not a protected classification.

23. A person who is suffering from alcoholism is protected under anti-discrimination law.

T

24. The purpose of the Americans with Disabilities Act (ADA) is to ensure equal access to public accommodations for disabled people.

T

25. A landlord must rent to a convicted drug dealer who no longer deals drugs.

F Law excludes those convicted of dealing drugs.

26. A person who is suffering with AIDS or who is HIV-positive is protected under antidiscrimination law.

T

27. Public accommodations are required to remove architectural and communication barriers when readily achievable.

T

28. A lender's prohibited practice of refusing to give loans secured by mortgages in a certain neighborhood or community because of the area's crime rate or racial or ethnic composition is known as steering.

F redlining

29. Blockbusting is also known as panic peddling or panic selling.

T

30. Failure to display the HUD equal housing opportunity poster can shift the burden of proof to a broker responding to a HUD complaint.

T

31. If a building requires all units to be occupied by tenants age 35 or older, the landlord may discriminate on the basis of familial status, refusing to rent to pregnant women or families with children.

F must be at least 80% of the units occupied by age 55+

32. It is a violation of fair housing laws to refuse to rent to qualified individuals simply because a child will be occupying the residence.

T

33. A landlord can refuse to allow a disabled tenant to make changes to a rental unit.

F must allow the changes but can require the tenant to return the unit to the same condition

34. A disabled tenant may make reversible changes at her own expense and without permission.

T

35. Homosexuals and students are covered under federal fair housing laws.

F Sexual orientation is protected on some local levels, but occupation is not protected.

| | | |
|---|---|---|
| 36. | Senior housing discriminates based on age. | F familial status |
| 37. | The Equal Credit Opportunity Act requires lenders to give written explanations of why credit was denied. | T |
| 38. | A lender may refuse to loan in an area based on crime rates. | F would be redlining |
| 39. | Minors are protected under ECOA. | F Minors are not allowed to enter into contracts or loans. |
| 40. | A lender may refuse to lend to someone who has retired as he might not live long enough to pay off the loan. | F Age discrimination is not permitted under ECOA. |
| 41. | A seller has refused to accept a full-price offer since it comes from a protected class. The broker could file a complaint and request the commission as damages. | T |
| 42. | ADA ensures private accommodations for the disabled. | F public |
| 43. | Earnest money is placed into the brokerage trust account upon receipt of an offer. | F upon acceptance, when the offer becomes a contract |
| 44. | A bank that turns down a seasoned creditworthy investor who wants to buy in a high-crime neighborhood is often an example of legal redlining. | F Redlining is never legal. |
| 45. | A broker against whom a discrimination claim has been filed will immediately have her license revoked. | F HUD will first investigate the claim. |
| 46. | A city broker who is listing a farm with irrigation rights may be practicing above his level of competency. | T |
| 47. | A seller wants to get the highest price that is reflective of the market. Broker 1 does a CMA and values the house at $100,000. Broker 2 does a CMA and values the house at $110,000. Broker 3 tells the seller she can sell the home for $120,000. The seller lists with broker 3. The home sells for $105,000. Broker 3 is guilty of negligence. | T and unethical behavior |
| 48. | The law that requires lending to a qualified person who is receiving public assistance is the Truth in Lending Act. | F Equal Credit Opportunity Act (ECOA) |
| 49. | Brokers are NOT allowed to keep personal and trust funds in the same account, as it would be too easy to commingle the funds. | T |
| 50. | Earnest money is deposited into the operations account. | F trust account |
| 51. | Trust funds can be held in non-demand accounts | F must be demand |
| 52. | It is acceptable for a real estate professional to complete and fill out forms even if she does NOT fully understand the form. | F must be competent |
| 53. | An owner selling his own property (FSBO) may advertise that the property will NOT be sold to families with children. | F may not use a broker or advertise |
| 54. | Money held in trust accounts may be used to cover the expenses of the brokerage firm to maintain the account. | F Broker must use the brokerage firm's money to maintain the account. |
| 55. | The difference between misrepresentation and fraud is the intention of the person. | T |
| 56. | A for sale by owner may refuse to sell the property to anyone with a different religion. | T |
| 57. | A new broker with no financial background or training should NOT sell commercial property. | T |

| | | |
|---|---|---|
| 58. | Brokers are obligated to do a CMA before offering a listing price. | T |
| 59. | Baptists, Iranians, Pueblo Indians, pregnant women, and a drug user in rehabilitation would all be covered under fair housing law. | T |
| 60. | An employing broker commingles trust funds if he deposits monies and rents received from a client's various properties in the same trust account. | F All trust funds are deposited in the same trust account. |
| 61. | Price-fixing is a violation of the Sherman Antitrust Act. | T |
| 62. | An employing broker is allowed to have side agreements, or independent contractor agreements, with his employed salespeople. | T |
| 63. | A real estate professional who hears discussions of commissions among other professionals should "shout and get out" of the area. | T |
| 64. | Antitrust laws are used to promote and maintain competition. | T |
| 65. | An independent contractor should have a written agreement with the firm, stating that the contractor will pay her own taxes and set her own schedule. | T |
| 66. | A broker acting as an employer is allowed to let her employees pay their own withholding taxes. | F must pay for employees |
| 67. | The length and terms of a home warranty are for one year after closing. | F determined by the contract with the warranty company |
| 68. | New home construction warranties would cover structural or roof failures after closing. | T |
| 69. | Stigmatized property laws are set at the federal level. | F state level |
| 70. | A salesperson working as an independent contractor would expect set hours, vacation, and taxes to be withheld from all paychecks. | F sets own hours and pays all expenses such as taxes or for vacations |
| 71. | A group of brokers setting fees for the area are in violation of Regulation Z. | F Sherman antitrust law |

# FINANCING

(Test questions: Salesperson 6; Broker 7)

| | | |
|---|---|---|
| **1.** | A subordination agreement can change the priority of mortgage liens. | T |
| **2.** | A lender for a loan over 75% LTV would require PMI. | F 80% LTV |
| **3.** | APR is associated with ECOA (Equal Credit Opportunity Act). | F APR is associated with the Truth in Lending Act. |
| **4.** | All FHA loans have the same rules regarding assumption. | F different rules based on date of origination |
| **5.** | VA loans, made at different times, might have different rules regarding assumability. | T |
| **6.** | The parents of a veteran may obtain a VA loan using their child's benefit. | F must be the veteran |
| **7.** | FHA and VA loans may have a prepayment penalty. | F may *NOT* have a prepayment penalty |
| **8.** | A partially amortized loan will have a larger balloon than a term loan. | F smaller, as some principal is paid each month |
| **9.** | The remaining principal balance on an assumed loan would be recorded on a closing statement as a credit to the seller and debit to the buyer. | F Debit to seller; credit to buyer. Remember: all loans are always a buyer credit. |
| **10.** | A borrower who pays a fixed monthly payment of principal and interest over the term of the loan, and then makes a large principal payment at the end, *MOST* likely had a fully amortized loan. | F partially amortized loan |
| **11.** | A partially amortized loan would likely require a balloon payment at the end of the term. | T |
| **12.** | Under the Equal Credit Opportunity Act, you cannot discriminate on the basis of sexual orientation. | F not protected under ECOA |
| **13.** | When a loan is sold in the secondary market, the borrower may be required to send the monthly payments to a different address. | T |
| **14.** | Most loan origination fees are tax deductible. | T |
| **15.** | A loan discount point is generally 1% of the sales price. | F loan amount |
| **16.** | All loans involve discount points. | F only if the interest is being bought down |
| **17.** | All types of mortgage loans, with the exception of assumed loans, would involve loan origination fees. | T |
| **18.** | In order to pledge lands, all owners must execute a security instrument. | T |
| **19.** | Written evidence of a promise to repay borrowed money is known as an acknowledgment. | F promissory note |
| **20.** | The security for a mortgage is a promissory note. | F Security for a note is a mortgage. |
| **21.** | A deed of trust creates a lien but does *NOT* convey title. | T |
| **22.** | The county commission in which the land is located governs the manner in which mortgage documents are recorded. | F State law governs. |

| | | |
|---|---|---|
| 23. | The lender of mortgage money is known as the mortgagee. | T |
| 24. | The clause in a mortgage that allows the lender to demand the unpaid balance in full on a default is called the escalator clause. | F acceleration clause |
| 25. | The advantage of leverage is that it requires a large down payment. | F small down payment |
| 26. | In a contract for deed, the seller transfers legal title to the buyer when the contract is signed. | F paid off |
| 27. | Leverage allows a relatively large return on a small cash investment. | T |
| 28. | A clause in a mortgage that allows a lender to declare a loan balance due on mortgage default is called an alienation clause. | F acceleration clause |
| 29. | A disadvantage to being highly leveraged is that the borrower is more likely to go into foreclosure. | T |
| 30. | If a buyer wants his loan to be assumable, he would ask for a due-on-sale clause. | F Due-on-sale clause requires full payment upon transfer of title. |
| 31. | A new FHA loan requires an appraisal and that there be no prepayment clause. | T |
| 32. | A clause in an existing note and mortgage states that a new buyer may not assume the mortgage without the lender's written permission. This clause is known as a prepayment clause. | F due-on-sale or alienation clause |
| 33. | When a property fails to sell at a mortgage foreclosure sale for an amount sufficient to satisfy a mortgage debt, the mortgagee may sue for a deficiency judgment. | T |
| 34. | Failure to meet an obligation when due is known as defeasance. | F default |
| 35. | The truth-in-lending law requires a good-faith estimate. | F RESPA |
| 36. | The proceeds from a foreclosure sale on mortgaged real property in excess of the mortgage indebtedness belong to the mortgagor. | T |
| 37. | In the event of default in the payment of a real estate mortgage loan, the lender may initiate condemnation proceedings. | F foreclosure |
| 38. | The borrower's right to redeem by paying all back payments, interest, and fees is called equitable redemption. | T |
| 39. | A deed of trust is similar to a deed. | F Deed of trust creates a lien; deed conveys title. |
| 40. | The written instrument that usually accompanies a mortgage is called a promissory note. | T |
| 41. | To find the remaining balance on a loan to be assumed, you would look at an amortization schedule. | T |
| 42. | A straight or interest-only loan will have a higher final payment than a partial or fully amortized loan. | T |
| 43. | The high bidder at a foreclosure sale will receive a deed. | T |
| 44. | Private mortgage insurance (PMI) allows the mortgagor to make a smaller down payment. | T |
| 45. | A lender that will NOT take a deed in lieu of foreclosure is most likely stopped because the property has junior liens. | T |
| 46. | Private mortgage insurance premiums are paid to insure the borrower against loss due to nonpayment. | F protects lenders against loss due to nonpayment |

| | | |
|---|---|---|
| 47. | A mortgage in which the interest rate is tied to an economic indicator is known as an index mortgage. | F adjustable-rate mortgage |
| 48. | An advantage of a term or straight mortgage is that there is no balloon at the end. | F The full amount of principal borrowed is due in a balloon payment. |
| 49. | The major advantage of contracting a mortgage for a term of 30 years rather than 25 years is the lower interest cost. | F lower monthly payment |
| 50. | A partially amortized loan will have a larger payment than an interest-only loan for the same amount. | T |
| 51. | A mortgage in which payments are established on a 25-year amortization schedule to be paid in full at the end of 10 years is an example of a home equity line of credit (HELOC). | F partially amortized |
| 52. | The payments in a partially amortized loan go toward the interest only. | F toward principal and interest |
| 53. | When a borrower can secure additional advances from the lender up to, but not exceeding, the original amount of the existing amortizing mortgage, she holds a package mortgage. | F line of credit |
| 54. | A loan that has equal monthly payments and is paid in full over the term of the loan is a term or straight loan. | F fully amortized |
| 55. | The balloon payment of an interest-only loan would be smaller than the balloon payment for a partial or fully amortized loan of the same amount. | F Larger since all principal is owed; fully amortized loans do not have balloons. |
| 56. | A loan is based on the sales price or appraised value, whichever is higher. | F whichever is lower |
| 57. | The reduction of a debt secured by a property through regular periodic payments is known as amortization. | T |
| 58. | The advantage of using a purchase-money mortgage is that it allows the buyer and seller to avoid paying a deed tax and recording fees. | F Avoids a loan origination fee and discount points. |
| 59. | A loan that provides for increases and decreases in the interest rate during its term is known as an escalated-rate loan. | F adjustable-rate loan |
| 60. | The value of property above the total liens or mortgages is known as equity. | T |
| 61. | The disadvantage of an interest-only loan is that no principal is paid over the term of the loan. | T |
| 62. | Charging in excess of the legally allowed rate of interest is known as exculpatory lending. | F usury |
| 63. | The disadvantage of leveraging is that the borrower has a higher risk. | T |
| 64. | A borrower who gives a mortgage to secure repayment of a loan is called a mortgagee. | F mortgagor |
| 65. | APR is the note rate plus all the closing costs to close the real estate transaction. | F note rate plus the cost of credit; RESPA is all closing costs |
| 66. | When a property is mortgaged, the mortgagee retains the usual rights of ownership. | F mortgagor |
| 67. | The term *debt service* refers to the payment of principal and interest. | T |

| | | |
|---|---|---|
| 68. | The value accepted by the lender for property pledged as collateral for a home loan is the sales price or appraised value, whichever is more. | F less |
| 69. | When making residential loans in excess of 80% loan-to-value ratio, conventional lenders usually require mortgage default insurance. | T |
| 70. | A blanket mortgage usually covers both personal and real property. | F package mortgage |
| 71. | A purchase-money mortgage allows the seller to retain title. | F conveys title |
| 72. | In a contract for deed, the seller gives the title, via deed, to the buyer when the buyer moves into the property. | F Seller holds the deed until the last payment has been made. |
| 73. | An FHA mortgage is an example of a conventional mortgage. | F Conventional mortgages do not have any government insurance or guarantee. |
| 74. | A partial release clause would be most likely found in a fully amortized loan. | F blanket mortgage |
| 75. | A blanket mortgage is one in which two or more properties are pledged as security for one mortgage debt. | T |
| 76. | A purchase-money mortgage is a loan involving a borrower, a construction lender, and any permanent lender. | F financing by the seller |
| 77. | A blanket loan is likely to contain a partial release clause. | T |
| 78. | When a borrower can secure an additional advance from the lender up to, but not exceeding, the original amount of the existing amortized mortgage, she holds a package mortgage. | F line of credit |
| 79. | A senior borrower who wants to access her equity without selling her house or making payments should get a home equity line of credit (HELOC). | F reverse mortgage |
| 80. | Usury laws are set at the state level. | T |
| 81. | A mortgage loan that calls for payments of interest only until the loan matures is an amortized loan. | F term or straight loan |
| 82. | A mortgage taken by a seller as partial payment for a property is called a sale-leaseback. | F purchase-money mortgage |
| 83. | Commercial banks like to make construction loans because these loans have a short life. | T |
| 84. | Exceeding the maximum interest rate is called usury. | T |
| 85. | A reverse mortgage provides for monthly payments from the mortgagor to the mortgagee. | F mortgagee to mortgagor |
| 86. | The clause in a mortgage that allows the borrower to pay off the mortgage early under specific terms and conditions is a prepayment clause. | T |
| 87. | A 3-day right of rescission would be given for a purchase of a second home. | F home equity loans or refinances |
| 88. | All real estate purchase loans have a three-day right of rescission. | F only home equity loans, second mortgages, and refinances |

| | | |
|---|---|---|
| 89. | A construction loan is an example of permanent financing that is also known as take-out. | F interim financing |
| 90. | Lenders may require a commitment for take-out before placing a construction loan. | T |
| 91. | A contractor will receive the proceeds of a construction loan in one lump sum at the time construction begins. | F Payments are made as work progresses. |
| 92. | FNMA buys FHA and VA mortgages. | T |
| 93. | The money for FHA loans is provided by any governmental agency. | F qualified lenders |
| 94. | Mortgage brokers act as intermediaries between lenders and borrowers. | T |
| 95. | The mortgagee's consent is necessary on completion of the sale of property with an existing VA or FHA loan that is being assumed. | T |
| 96. | A subprime loan typically has a higher interest rate and is more likely to default. | T |
| 97. | Real estate professionals should make sure the buyer and seller fully understand the risks of seller financing. | T |
| 98. | FNMA was established primarily for the purpose of buying existing loans from lending institutions in order to stabilize the mortgage market. | T |
| 99. | FNMA insures mortgages through insurance fees paid by borrowers. | F buys mortgages |
| 100. | Points charged by a lender at the time of loan origination increase the time over which the loan will be repaid. | F increase lender's yield |
| 101. | Points, origination, interest, and taxes are deductible on income taxes. | T |
| 102. | The note rate is typically higher than the APR. | F APR is higher since it is the note rate plus the cost of credit. |
| 103. | The appraised value of a property, for which a veteran has applied for a VA loan, is lower than the contract price. In this situation, the veteran may pay the difference between the appraised value and the contract price in cash. | T |
| 104. | VA loans can be assumed by nonveterans. | T |
| 105. | A borrower at a new loan closing would sign a deed. | F note and deed of trust or mortgage |
| 106. | FHA makes mortgage loans directly to consumers. | F insures loans |
| 107. | The purpose of FHA and private mortgage insurance is to protect the lender against deficiency in the event of foreclosure. | T |
| 108. | When an FHA loan is secured to purchase a house, the origination fee on the loan would usually be paid by the buyer. | T |
| 109. | Funds for FHA-insured home loans are usually supplied by the Federal Housing Administration. | F by qualified lending institutions |
| 110. | A new FHA loan may be made to a borrower whose intent is to rent the entire property for which the loan is obtained. | F must be owner-occupied |
| 111. | A new VA loan may be made to a qualified veteran whose intent is to rent the entire property for which the loan is obtained. | F must be owner-occupied |

| | |
|---|---|
| 112. A bank looks at FHA as an insurance agency. | T |
| 113. Points are charged to increase the lender's yield. | T |
| 114. In a tight money market, buyers may have to pay more discount points for financing of real estate. | T |
| 115. As specified by the federal Truth in Lending Act, attorneys' fees are components of the annual percentage rate of a finance charge. | F  not a finance charge |
| 116. The true cost of credit is reflected by the points. | F  APR |
| 117. Per regulation Z, lenders must disclose the APR when advertising. | T |
| 118. The purpose of the Truth in Lending Act is to establish maximum charges for credit. | F  doesn't set charges |
| 119. In a real estate advertisement that includes information on mortgage financing, it is legally permissible to say "liberal terms available to qualified buyer" without further information given. | T |
| 120. An ad that states, "Great terms, low down payment, and check out our pricing" would trigger the full disclosure requirement of Regulation Z. | F general terms are OK, but specific terms require disclosure |
| 121. Discount points on an FHA-insured loan are paid by either the buyer or the seller. | T |
| 122. The Truth in Lending Act designates the maximum amount of closing costs that lenders can charge borrowers for securing new loans. | F  requires disclosures; doesn't limit charges |
| 123. The purpose of APR is to allow borrowers to compare credit costs. | T |
| 124. Lenders must give borrowers a 3-day right of rescission on home purchase loans. | F  only on refinance and home equity loans |
| 125. Value today – Purchase price = Equity | F Value today – Debt today = Equity |
| 126. A broker advertises real property as follows: "Financing available with 15% down payment." This statement does *NOT* trigger full disclosure under the Truth in Lending Act. | F requires disclosure since it offers specific terms |
| 127. The Truth in Lending Act and Regulation Z apply to loans to businesses. | F  loans to individuals |
| 128. The Truth in Lending Act is included in the Consumer Credit Protection Act. | T |

QST  **The Truth in Lending Act and Regulation Z:**

| | |
|---|---|
| 129. Regulate interest rates | F  advertising of interest rates |
| 130. Require full disclosure of the full real estate loan costs | T |
| 131. Designate the maximum amount of closing costs a lender may charge borrowers for securing new loans | F |
| 132. Require that lenders must disclose the best financing terms | F  all terms of financing |
| 133. Require disclosure of the annual percentage rate (APR) | T |
| 134. Require disclosure of the prime rate | F nominal and annual percentage rate (APR) |
| 135. Regulate mortgage loans on commercial properties | F |

| | | |
|---|---|---|
| **136.** Apply to brokers when they quote or advertise interest rates for mortgage loan funds | T | |
| **137.** Require lenders to disclose all closing costs for the transaction | F lender costs; RESPA discloses all closing costs | |

**QST    According to the Truth in Lending Act (Regulation Z), the following wording in an advertisement would trigger full disclosure:**

| | |
|---|---|
| **138.** Nominal interest rate of 8% | T |
| **139.** 10% down payment | T |
| **140.** Low down payment | F General terms, sales price, and APR do *NOT* trigger full disclosure. |
| **141.** Annual percentage rate 6.5% | F APR or price okay |
| **142.** 20 easy monthly installments | T |
| **143.** Ms. Thomas is selling her house and accepting a second mortgage for $5,000 at 10% for 5 years. Under the Truth in Lending Act/Regulation Z, she is required to report the APR and the finance charges to the buyer. | F Individual sellers need not disclose. |
| **144.** RESPA requires that home equity loans have a 3-day right of rescission. | F Truth in Lending Act |
| **145.** APR reflects the true cost of obtaining credit. | T |
| **146.** RESPA requires lenders to disclose all closing costs in a HUD-1 within 1 week of loan application. | F within 3 days in a good-faith estimate |
| **147.** Fully amortized loans will require the full payment of principal at the end. | F term/straight or partially amortized |
| **148.** Partially amortized loans have monthly payments of principal and interest. | T |
| **149.** The clause in a mortgage that allows the lender to demand loan repayment if a borrower sells the property is the defeasance clause. | F alienation/due-on-sale clause |
| **150.** A financial arrangement by which a buyer purchases property using borrowed funds but does *NOT* actually receive title to the property until after the loan has been fully repaid, is a land contract. | T |
| **151.** A lender who wants to make sure that a borrower will be legally obligated to pay off the entire unpaid loan balance if the borrower defaults on the payments should use an acceleration clause. | T |
| **152.** When a property is sold in a foreclosure proceeding, and the sale does *NOT* bring sufficient funds to cover the senior mortgages, the original mortgagor may be subject to a default judgment. | F deficiency |
| **153.** PMI is *MOST* often required for loans over 80% LTV. | T |
| **154.** Annual percentage rate (APR) is lower than the nominal interest rate. | F higher, as it includes the nominal/note rate plus costs of credit |
| **155.** LTV is used to determine the amount the lender will loan and if the borrower will have to pay PMI. | T |

156. The acceleration clause would be used to stop the loan from being assumed in the future.

F due-on-sale/alienation

157. Amortized loans allow for periodic payments of interest only, with the principal due as a lump-sum payment at maturity.

F term/straight loans

158. FNMA is a participant in the secondary mortgage market.

T

159. A conventional loan is *NEVER* insured.

F The lender may require private mortgage insurance for loans with an 80% or higher LTV.

**QST   Characteristics of a Federal Housing Administration (FHA) loan are:**

160. The LTV is typically lower than conventional loans.

F higher

161. The lender is insured against the loss.

T

162. Loans must *NOT* have a prepayment clause.

T

163. Assumption requires the lender's approval.

T for loans originated after 1989

164. When applying for the original loan the property must be appraised by a FHA-approved appraiser.

T

165. A good-faith estimate of closing costs is required to be delivered by closing.

F

166. In a PITI payment, the principal and insurance are deductible on income taxes.

F interest and taxes

167. Funds for VA loans usually are provided by the secondary mortgage market.

F approved lenders

168. A promissory note creates the security for a lien.

F It is just a promise to pay.

169. A veteran buys a home with a VA-guaranteed loan. Two years later, the veteran sells his home to a buyer who, with the lender's approval, assumes the veteran's loan. Since the buyer is approved, the veteran is no longer financially responsible if the buyer defaults 6 months later.

T

170. If discount points are charged on an FHA loan, they are paid by either the buyer or the seller.

T

171. It is acceptable under the Real Estate Settlement Procedures Act (RESPA) to charge excessive escrow amounts for payments of taxes, insurance, and other charges.

F no excessive fees

172. The RESPA HUD-1 closing statement must be given at loan application or within 3 days.

F closing

173. The RESPA closing statement includes all loan charges and other closing costs involved in the closing of a sale.

T

174. RESPA requires that an applicant for a mortgage loan receive a good-faith estimate of closing costs from the lender at application.

F at application or no later than 3 days after

175. RESPA applies to all properties of five or more units.

F government-related loans for one to four units

176. The annual percentage rate (APR) takes into account the nominal interest rate and finance charges.

T

177. RESPA applies to transactions involving commercial and industrial loans.

F residential properties of four units or less

178. A disadvantage of accepting a deed in lieu of foreclosure is that the mortgagee takes title subject to any junior or secondary liens.

T

179. When mortgagees take a deed in lieu of foreclosure, they are guaranteed a title free of encumbrances.

F Might take on junior/secondary liens.

180. If a buyer in a real estate transaction makes a deposit and agrees to pay the seller a certain monthly sum toward the balance due on the contract, and the seller retains legal title, the buyer has entered into a package money mortgage.

F contract for deed

181. An installment land contract normally provides the buyer with legal title at the closing.

F Equitable title seller holds legal title until paid in full.

182. In an installment land contract sale, the deed will usually be delivered when the contract terms are satisfied.

T

183. The disadvantage of leverage is that it requires a small down payment.

F The disadvantage is small owner equity and a larger debt.

# FINANCE MATH

1. Mr. Jones borrowed $40,000 on July 1 at 13% interest to purchase a home. The loan was amortized over a 30-year period with a monthly payment of $442.80 for principal and interest. What is the portion of the first payment that applies to interest?

   $40,000 \times 0.13 = \$5,200; \$5,200 \div 12 = \mathbf{\$433.33}$

2. A short-term loan requires an escrow of 3 months' payment at closing. If the loan amount is $650,000 at 7.5% interest, how much escrow is needed?

   $650,000 \times 0.075 = \$48,750 \div 12$ (to get monthly interest) $= \$4,062.50 \times 3 = \mathbf{\$12,187.50}$ **to meet the 3-month requirement**

3. The lender will allow a monthly payment equal to 25% of the borrower's income. The payment is $800. How much is the borrower's monthly income?

   Monthly payment of $800 \times 4 = \mathbf{\$3,200}$, or $800 \div 0.25$; backwards, $3,200 \times 0.25 = \$800$

4. A home is sold for $63,000. If an 80% loan-to-value ratio were used, 5 discount points would be how much?

   $63,000 \times 0.8 = \$50,400; \$50,400 \times 0.05 = \mathbf{\$2,520}$

5. On a $65,000 property, the buyer obtains a loan with an 80% loan-to-value ratio at 16% interest, 20-year amortization, and 3 points. How much will the lender receive for the discount?

   $65,000 \times 0.8 = \$52,000; \$52,000 \times 0.03 = \mathbf{\$1,560}$

6. The loan-to-value ratio is 85% on a $110,000 property. If 4 points are required by the lender, the dollar amount of the points is how much?

   $110,000 \times 0.85 = \$93,500; \$93,500 \times 0.04 = \mathbf{\$3,740}$

7. A property using straight-line depreciation of 39 years is valued at $300,000. How much depreciation has been taken after 15 years?

   $300,000 \div 39 \times 15 = \mathbf{\$115,384.62}$

8. A couple who earns $4,840 per month after taxes wants to make a mortgage payment of no more than 25% of their monthly earnings. Using the amortization table below, determine which interest rate and term will give the couple the payment closest to what they are seeking.

   The first step is to determine the amount of the payment. $4,840 \times 0.25 = \$1,210$. Using the amortization chart, a loan at **6.25% for 20 years**, which is a payment of $1,206.03, is the closest to what the couple is seeking.

| Interest | 10 Years | 15 years | 20 Years | 30 Years |
|---|---|---|---|---|
| 5.00% | $1,750.08 | $1,304.81 | $1,088.93 | $885.76 |
| 5.25% | $1,770.31 | $1,326.40 | $1,111.84 | $911.14 |
| 5.50% | $1,790.68 | $1,348.19 | $1,135.01 | $936.85 |
| 5.75% | $1,811.19 | $1,370.18 | $1,158.44 | $962.90 |
| 6.00% | $1,831.84 | $1,392.36 | $1,182.11 | $989.26 |
| 6.25% | $1,852.62 | $1,414.75 | $1,206.03 | $1,015.93 |
| 6.50% | $1,873.54 | $1,437.33 | $1,230.20 | $1,042.91 |
| 6.75% | $1,894.60 | $1,460.10 | $1,254.60 | $1,070.19 |
| 7.00% | $1,915.79 | $1,483.07 | $1,279.24 | $1,097.75 |

9. Using the table above, what would be the difference in monthly payments for a 6.5% loan for 20 years and a 7% loan for 30?

The monthly loan payment at 6.5% is $1,230.20 and the 7% monthly loan payment is 1,097.75. The difference is $132.45.

10. A borrower who wants to pay up to but no more than $1,400 per month should use what terms?

6% for 15 years

# VALUATION AND MARKET ANALYSIS

(Test questions: Salesperson 8; Broker 6)

| | | |
|---|---|---|
| 1. | Outdated lighting fixtures would likely be an example of incurable functional obsolescence. | F curable |
| 2. | A six-bedroom home with one bathroom would be an example of functional obsolescence. | T |
| 3. | A severely damaged foundation would likely be an example of incurable physical deterioration. | T |
| 4. | Under the principle of regression, a four-bedroom house would likely lose value if located in a neighborhood comprising smaller, less valuable properties. | T |
| 5. | Under the principle of progression, a $50,000 property would likely gain value if located in a neighborhood comprising much more expensive properties. | T |
| 6. | Under the principle of conformity, a property with a modest house would lose value if surrounded by properties with significantly larger homes. | F  Property values will tend toward the surroundings, so a modest house would gain value in this instance. |
| 7. | It is the function of the appraiser to establish market price. | F  estimate market value |
| 8. | Functional obsolescence is identified with heavy street traffic in a residential area. | F  economic obsolescence |
| 9. | Depreciation is one of the elements of value. | F  demand |
| 10. | In an appraisal using the sales comparison approach, adjustments for differences in characteristics are made to the comparable property. | T |
| 11. | Income, capitalized value, demand, and depreciation are the four essential elements of value. | F  demand, utility, scarcity, and transferability (DUST) |
| 12. | A determination of highest and best use is found in both a CMA and the appraisal. | F  only an appraisal |
| 13. | Increasing rents in an area can be explained by the principle of highest and best use. | F  supply and demand |
| 14. | The essential worth of any property is determined by the assessed value. | F  market value |
| 15. | Data needed to apply the sales comparison approach can be gathered from public records and multiple listing services. | T |
| 16. | The MOST common approach to the valuation of residential property is the income approach. | F  sales comparison approach |
| 17. | Physical, local, economic, and social are the four elements of value. | F  demand, utility, scarcity, and transferability (DUST) |
| 18. | A building with an outdated design would be identified with functional obsolescence. | T |
| 19. | The probable price a property will bring in a competitive and open market where all conditions required of a fair sale are met is called market price. | F  market value |

| | | |
|---|---|---|
| **20.** | Replacement cost is the present cost of replacing an improvement with another having the same utility. | T |
| **21.** | Reproduction cost is the present cost of reproducing an improvement with the same or highly similar materials. | T |
| **22.** | An appraiser estimated the value of a property by carefully checking the prices of comparable properties that were recently sold. This method is an example of the cost approach. | F  sales comparison approach |
| **23.** | Demand, utility, scarcity, and transferability are elements of value. | T  DUST |
| **24.** | A comparative market analysis is similar to the cost approach to value. | F  sales comparison approach |
| **25.** | Real estate salespeople and broker associates can do appraisals. | F  only licensed appraisers |
| **26.** | The highest and best use of any parcel of real estate may change with the passage of time. | T |
| **27.** | The principle of substitution underlies the sales comparison approach to value. | T  substitution underlies all approaches |
| **28.** | The market value of a residential property is likely to decrease if a zoning change to permit light industry in the area is planned. | T |
| **29.** | Market value is the price, in terms of cash or its equivalent, on which a willing buyer and seller will agree, where neither is under any undue pressure and both are typically motivated, have adequate knowledge, and are acting in their own best interest. | T |
| **30.** | The principle of substitution underlies all approaches to value. | T |
| **31.** | When taking a listing on a two-story home, salesperson John wants to measure its square footage. The square footage will be based on exterior dimensions and then multiplied by 2. | T |
| **32.** | A home that is under a flight path from a local airport suffers from functional obsolescence. | F  external obsolescence |
| **33.** | In estimating the value of a property, air pollution, zoning restrictions, and the character of the neighborhood could be considered factors of economic (external) obsolescence. | T |
| **34.** | The sales comparison approach to value is used to indicate the value in relation to recent sales activity. | T |
| **35.** | CMAs are used to determine the listing price and have no value to buyers. | F  Buyers use a CMA to determine what to offer. |
| **36.** | The term *replacement cost new* as used in the cost approach means the present cost of replacing the subject with another having the same utility. | T |
| **37.** | A broker is performing a competitive market analysis to determine a listing price for a single-family house. If comparable properties are in worse overall condition than the seller's house, the sales prices of the comparables should be increased. | T |
| **38.** | Rotting wood is an example of functional obsolescence. | F  physical deterioration |
| **39.** | The approach to value that makes adjustments to recently sold comparables is the income approach. | F  sales comparison approach |

| | | |
|---|---|---|
| 40. | A broker may charge for a BPO but should make clear it is not an appraisal. | T |
| 41. | When using the cost approach to value while appraising a small department store, the appraiser will need to determine the current cost of constructing the improvements. | T |
| 42. | In an appraisal, the value of a fireplace is determined by how much it costs to purchase and install. | F determined by what homes with and without fireplaces sell for in the area |
| 43. | Reproduction cost refers to the cost to replace an improvement with equivalent utility and replacement cost refers to the cost to build a replica. | F Reproduction is a replica; replacement is equal utility. |
| 44. | A BPO completed by a salesperson or broker may be used for appraisal purposes. | F must clearly note it is not an appraisal |
| 45. | Kelly is performing a market analysis on a residence. Because of the differences between similar properties and the subject property, Kelly should take into account the seller's original cost to build. | F recently sold comparables |
| 46. | Langley is appraising a 25-year-old residence. The best indicator of market value is MOST likely to be found by using the income approach. | F sales comparison approach |
| 47. | A property owner has a house on a busy intersection. He demolishes the house and builds a convenience store on the site. His decision was MOST likely based on the principle of highest and best use. | T |
| 48. | Topography, zoning, environmental issues, and building codes have an effect on real estate value. | T |
| 49. | James built a $150,000 home in a neighborhood where the average price range is $60,000–$75,000. James's home value will suffer due to progression. | F regression |
| 50. | Rapidly changing markets often require the appraiser to adjust for the date of sale. | T |
| 51. | In utilizing the cost approach, the appraiser considers the depreciated value of the land. | F Land is not depreciated; only the improvements are. |
| 52. | An appraiser uses the sales comparison approach to determine the cost to reproduce a property. | F cost approach |
| 53. | A broker completing a CMA should use comparable sales from 12 to 18 months ago. | F 6 months to no longer than 1 year |
| 54. | Net operating income is used as part of the income approach. | T |
| 55. | An appraiser's compensation must be based on a percentage of the subject property's appraised value. | F must NOT |
| 56. | When determining the value of a fireplace or other amenities, the cost of the fireplace plus installation determines value. | F Comparison of sold properties with and without a fireplace determines the value of amenities. |
| 57. | Economic/locational obsolescence is considered an external force. | T |

| | | |
|---|---|---|
| 58. | A single-family home has been deemed to depreciate $10,000 because of a factory in the neighborhood. This is an example of functional obsolescence. | F  external/locational/economic obsolescence |
| 59. | An appraiser would use the income approach as the MOST reliable approach to estimate the value of a 70-year-old church. | F  cost approach |
| 60. | Capitalization is used to determine the value of unique properties. | F  income properties |
| 61. | Physical depreciation is MOST frequently associated with ordinary wear and tear. | T |
| 62. | The computational technique using capitalization of income is to predict future value. | F predict present value |
| 63. | Deprecation is the loss of value from outside influences. | F  loss of value from any cause |
| 64. | An outdated heating system is an example of functional obsolescence. | T |
| 65. | The reproduction cost approach to value would give the MOST accurate appraisal of a new property. | T |
| 66. | When large quantities of houses are available for sale, the price will decrease. However, if houses are relatively scarce and desired, the price will increase. This is an example of contribution. | F  supply and demand |
| 67. | In addition to licensing, appraisers may have additional designations such as MAI or SRA. | T |
| 68. | An appraiser considers a comparable sale property's current condition and usefulness of the structure to estimate its effective age. | T |

**QST   The elements or characteristics required for a property to have value include:**

| | | |
|---|---|---|
| 69. | Demand | T |
| 70. | Scarcity | T |
| 71. | Depreciation | F  part of the cost approach |
| 72. | Transferability | T |
| 73. | Conformity | F  a principle of value not an element of value |

**QST   According to the definition of market value:**

| | | |
|---|---|---|
| 74. | Both buyer and seller must be well informed. | T |
| 75. | Market value is the average price that a property will bring. | F  probable price |
| 76. | Both buyer and seller must act without undue pressure. | T |
| 77. | Payment must be made in cash or its equivalent. | T |
| 78. | When the price of residential real estate in an area is declining, the principle that would best explain the decline is contribution. | F supply and demand |
| 79. | You look at four similar houses for sale in the same area and choose the house with the lowest asking price. You probably are basing your decision on the principle of conformity. | F  principle of substitution |

| | |
|---|---|
| 80. A builder developed a subdivision in which the demand for homes was great. He sold the last lot in his subdivision for a much higher price than he had sold the first lot in the area. This illustrates the principle of supply and demand. | T |
| 81. In appraising a special-purpose building such as a post office, the MOST reliable approach to an indication of its value would generally be the sales comparison approach. | F cost approach |
| 82. Economic obsolescence results from an inharmonious land use in a neighborhood. | T |
| 83. Depreciation generally applies to both the land and the building. | F building only |
| 84. The gross rent multiplier method is used in the cost approach. | F income approach |
| 85. In order to determine the value of an income property, the appraiser must determine the net operating income. | T |
| 86. An airport routing was changed, with the result being that airplanes flew over a residential area. The subsequent loss in value caused by the airplane noise would best be described as economic obsolescence. | T |

**QST    In the sales comparison approach to value, the appraiser would consider:**

| | |
|---|---|
| 87. Annual gross income | F income approach |
| 88. Conditions under which a comparable property was sold | T |
| 89. Replacement cost | F cost approach |
| 90. Original cost | F never a consideration in determining value |
| 91. Physical characteristics | T |
| 92. Location | T |
| 93. Date of sale in a rapidly depreciating neighborhood | T |
| 94. An individual built her dream house for $300,000 in a neighborhood of $100,000 homes and suffered a substantial loss when she had to sell four years later. This is an example of the principle of regression. | T |
| 95. The final step in the valuation process is to average the value estimates arrived at from the sales comparison, cost, and income approaches. | F Final step is reconciliation (and never an average). |
| 96. When an appraiser analyzes and weighs estimates of value from appropriate approaches, the process is known as reconciliation. | T |
| 97. The principle of value that determines if something is financially feasible is conformity. | F contribution |
| 98. Averaging may NOT be used in any phase of appraisal. | T |
| 99. The sales comparison approach can also be called the summation approach. | F market data approach |
| 100. In the sales comparison approach, adjustments are made to the subject. | F never to the subject; always to the comparables |

101. When using the sales comparison approach in a quickly increasing market, an appraiser might make an adjustment for the time or date of sale.

T

102. Reproduction and replacement are used in the income approach.

F cost

103. Another name for the cost approach is summation.

T

104. The income approach would be the *BEST* way to value a unique or special-use property.

F cost

105. To value a shopping center, the *BEST* approach would be sales comparison.

F income

106. A competitive market analysis uses principles similar to the cost approach to determine value.

F sales comparison

107. The formula for a gross rent multiplier is: Value ÷ Rent = GRM.

T

108. A large GRM of 200 would be a monthly multiplier and would need monthly rental income to determine value.

T

109. The formula to determine value with IRV is NOI × Cap rate = Value.

F NOI ÷ Cap rate = Value

110. The formula to determine value with GRM is GRM ÷ Rent = Value.

F GRM × Rent = Value

111. When using a GRM, the type of multiplier must match the rent income (annual-to-annual or month-to-month).

T

112. A small GRM of 15 would be an annual multiplier and would need monthly rents to determine value.

F annual rents

113. In estimating the market value of an income-producing property, an appraiser should consider the sales price of the subject property.

F would use the net operating income, not sales comparison

114. All federally related loans require appraisals.

T

115. The *BEST* way to determine value is by doing a CMA or BPO.

F an appraisal

116. A buyer who wants to know what amount to offer should get an appraisal.

F CMA

117. A regional market has declined 20% in the last year. A broker or appraiser does *NOT* need to take this into consideration since the decline impacts the entire area.

F would need to make time of sale adjustment to all sales over a month old

118. Appraisal requirements are set at a state level only.

F federal and state

119. Four homes have sold in the area in the last year. The first home to sell is the *BEST* for determining the value of the neighborhood.

F The most recent sale is the best for determining current value.

120. Increasing returns mean a loss in value, while decreasing returns mean an increase in value.

F increasing = increase in value; decreasing = decrease in value

# VALUATION MATH

1. A business property is valued at $100,000. To earn a capitalization rate of 9% of the total investment, the property should return a monthly income of how much?

   (V) $100,000 × (R) 9% = (I) $9,000; $9,000 ÷ 12 = **$750** monthly income

2. Samuel Sims, an appraiser, discovered that comparable houses were selling at the rate of $31 per square foot of living area, plus $9,700 for the lot value. If the subject property measures 24 feet by 52 feet and is two stories high, what would be his estimate of value?

   24 × 52 = 1,248; 1,248 × 2 = 2,496 sq ft living area; 2,496 × $31 = $77,376 house value; $77,376 + $9,700 = **$87,076**

3. What capitalization rate should be used to estimate the value of a subject property?

   A: $49,000 ÷ $376,923 = 0.**13**

   B: $50,000 ÷ $384,615 = 0.**13**

   C: $51,000 ÷ $392,308 = 0.**13** **(13%)**

|  | Comparable A | Comparable B | Comparable C |
|---|---|---|---|
| Gross income | $102,000 | $105,000 | $107,100 |
| Effective income | $ 98,000 | $100,000 | $102,000 |
| Net operating income | $ 49,000 | $ 50,000 | $ 51,000 |
| Selling price | $376,923 | $384,615 | $392,308 |

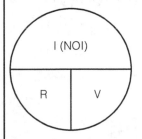

4. An apartment building has an annual gross income of $70,000 and operating expenses of $40,000. If the capitalization rate is 10.5%, what is the market value?

   $70,000 – $40,000 = $30,000 net; $30,000 ÷ 0.105 = **$285,714.29**

5. A property produces $9,700 income per year. Management fees are $650 per year, and monthly heating costs are $102. If the property is valued at $78,260, what is the owner's capitalization rate?

   $102 × 12 = $1,224 annual heat; $1,224 + $650 = $1,874 operating expense; $9,700 – $1,874 = $7,826 net; $7,826 ÷ $78,260 = 0.1 **(10%)**

6. A rectangular lot 175 feet by 300 feet is sold at $1.75 per square foot. The brokerage fee is 10%. How much is the fee?

   300 ft × 175 ft, = 52,500 sq ft; 52,500 × $1.75 = $91,875; $91,875 × 0.1 = **$9,187.50**

7. The market value of a property is $147,400. If properties are assessed at 60% of market value and the tax rate is $51.47 per $1,000, what is the property tax bill?

   $147,400 × 0.6 = $88,440; $88,440 ÷ 1,000 = 88.44; 88.44 × $51.47 = **$4,552**

8. A restaurant has a gross annual income of $400,000 and an operating expense ratio of 80%. If the capitalization rate is 12.5%, what is the value?

   $400,000 – 320,000 (80%) = $80,000 NOI $80,000 ÷ 0.125 = **$640,000**

9. A property has a gross rent multiplier of 200. The annual net income from rent was $24,000. What is the value of the property?

200 × $2,000 ($24,000 ÷ 12 = $2,000 monthly) = **$400,000**

10. If you own a building worth $225,000, what monthly net income is necessary to give you a 15% return?

$225,000 × 0.15 = $33,750 annual net; $33,750 ÷ 12 = **$2,812.50**

11. An appraiser is estimating the value of a building that has a net income of $5,000 per quarter and a capitalization rate of 8%. The value of this property is $250,000.

T (I) $5,000 × 4 = $20,000 ÷ (R) 0.08 = **$250,000**

12. An appraiser is using the gross rent multiplier (GRM) method to estimate the market value of a single-family home. The GRM is 200, and the annual rents are $12,000. The value of the property is $200,000.

T 200 × $1,000 ($12,000 ÷ 12 = $1,000) = **$200,000**

13. The GRM is determined by the value times the rent.

F Value ÷ Rent = GRM

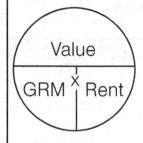

14. The annual net income for an office building is $20,000. If the owner realizes a 9% return on his investment, the value of the building is $285,714.

F (I) $20,000 ÷ (R) 0.09 =(V) **$222,222**

15. A broker is asked by the buyer what the price per square foot is of the property, which is listed for $350,000 and has 1,800 square feet. The price per square foot is $150.

F **$194.44**

# PROPERTY OWNERSHIP

(Test questions: Salesperson 7; Broker 6)

1.  Upon the death of a life tenant, the estate passes to the life tenant's heirs.

    F  passes to the reverter or the remainderman, or their heirs, who will have fee simple absolute interest

2.  An owner-occupant in a cooperative might own the unit in fee simple.

    F  owns shares in the corporation and receives proprietary lease

3.  An owner-occupant in a condominium might own the unit in fee simple.

    T

4.  Land can be considered a fixture.

    F  Fixtures are attached to improvements, which are attached to the land.

5.  Depreciation allowance on personal income taxes is one of the advantages of owning real estate.

    T

6.  Land is generally considered a liquid asset.

    F  Land takes too long to sell to be considered a liquid asset.

7.  One disadvantage of investing in real estate is its lack of liquidity.

    T

8.  Mortgage interest, property taxes, and property insurance premiums are all tax deductible.

    F  Insurance premiums are not deductible (remember POIT).

9.  A brother and sister are buying property together. The brother is planning to live in the house with his wife and pay rent to his sister for her share in the property. The licensee should advise the siblings to take title as tenants in common.

    F  Licensee should advise the siblings to consult an attorney.

10. Real estate property tax liens take priority over all other liens.

    T

11. Mortgage liens take priority over all other liens.

    F  Tax liens have priority.

12. A husband and wife own a property as joint tenants. The husband's will leaves his share in the property to their daughter. Upon the death of the husband, the surviving wife and daughter will own the property as tenants in common.

    F  The wife will own the property in severalty. The will is irrelevant since title was taken in joint tenancy.

13. The term *appurtenances* can include improvements.

    T  any right, interest, privilege, or improvement that runs with the land

14. In determining if an item affixed to real property is a fixture, one of the factors to consider is the intention of the party attaching the item.

    T

15. A shared driveway would qualify as an easement in gross.

    F  easement appurtenant

16. A buyer or seller who discovers an encroachment before or after closing should consult an attorney.

    T

17. Mr. Jones, whose wife recently died, hesitated to renew his lease in anticipation of moving to his daughter's home. If he continued to pay rent after the expiration date on his lease, he would be considered a periodic tenant.

    T

| | | |
|---|---|---|
| **18.** | A consideration in determining whether or not an object is a fixture includes the adaptation of the object. | T |
| **19.** | To protect against an encroachment, the purchaser should obtain title insurance. | F survey or an ILC (improvement location certificate) |
| **20.** | Mr. Smith leases a restaurant to Mr. Jones for 5 years. Jones installs his own ovens, booths, counters, and other equipment. These items are considered personal property and can be removed at the end of the lease. | T |
| **21.** | Liens are considered encumbrances. | T Encumbrances are imperfections or clouds on title. |
| **22.** | A life estate has a duration of no more than 50 years. | F someone's lifetime |
| **23.** | The sellers removed the attached microwave, which had *NOT* been excluded in the sale. The sellers are in breach. | T |
| **24.** | A person who has not been paid for work performed on real estate may file a lien and foreclose. | T mechanic's lien |
| **25.** | A shared driveway and a party wall are both examples of easements in gross. | F easements appurtenant |
| **26.** | A remainderman has the legal right to possess the property of a life tenant. | F Remainderman has a future possession interest. |
| **27.** | A farmer who rents 300 acres under a 10-year lease holds a leasehold estate. | T |
| **28.** | A fee simple owner of land has maximum control of the use of her land. | T |
| **29.** | The right of ingress and egress over the land of another is classified as an encroachment. | F easement—ingress is right to enter; egress is right to exit |
| **30.** | The right of an owner to occupy a parcel of real estate forever is called a life estate. | F fee simple absolute estate |
| **31.** | A storage building that extends over the boundary line between the property of the building's owner and an adjacent property is an example of encroachment. | T |
| **32.** | Failure of a homeowner to pay for labor and materials to repair the home may result in a mechanic's lien. | T |
| **33.** | Two individuals share ownership in an arrangement wherein if one owner dies, his interest goes to his heirs. This is an example of joint tenancy. | F tenancy in common |
| **34.** | Ownership of private property by an individual is described as severalty. | T |
| **35.** | Two friends decide to purchase property as co-owners. In order to protect their heirs' rights of inheritance, they should take title to the property as joint tenants. | F tenants in common |
| **36.** | A young couple has agreed to purchase a property. The closing date is scheduled just prior to the couple's marriage date. The broker should advise them to take title as joint tenants. | F Never advise as to form of ownership. |

| | |
|---|---|
| 37. John and Sue own a property as joint tenants. John has named his son to inherit the property upon John's death. When John dies, the property will go to his son. | F Joint tenancy overrides a will. |
| 38. Tom, Sally, and Jim all own a property as tenants in common. The responsibility for paying the property tax is based on shares of ownership. | F Tenants in common have a joint AND individual obligation to pay the property taxes. |
| 39. Ms. Hidalgo and Ms. Moore hold title to a duplex as joint tenants. If Ms. Moore dies, Ms. Hidalgo would receive Ms. Moore's interests. | T |
| 40. Two friends purchase property and wish to protect their rights of inheritance. They should take title as tenants in common. | T |
| 41. Real estate owed by an entity, such as a corporation, is held as tenants in common. | F severalty |
| 42. A limited partner has risk equal to all of the other partners. | F limited to the amount invested |
| 43. In a general partnership, all partners have equal say and liability. | T |
| 44. In the transfer of real property, mineral rights may be reserved by the seller. | T |
| 45. An estate at sufferance is the estate with the lowest status. | T |
| 46. The recipient of an easement appurtenant enjoys an increase in the amount of property owned. | F increase in property value |
| 47. An easement by prescription is a right acquired by an adverse user for limited use or enjoyment of the land of another. | T |
| 48. Sole and separate ownership of real property is associated with joint tenancy. | F severalty |
| 49. Jordan's lease to Linda has 3 years remaining. He sells to Quinn, who takes title subject to the lease. | T |
| 50. A disadvantage to joint tenancy is that it has to go through probate before title can pass. | F Title passes immediately to the other cotenant(s). Tenants in common and severalty must go through probate. |
| 51. An easement is an example of an encumbrance that could change the physical condition of real estate. | T |
| 52. Rights, improvements, and privileges are examples of appurtenances. | T |
| 53. Easements appurtenant have only a dominant property. | F dominant and servient property |
| 54. The best form of ownership to recommend for married couples is joint tenancy. | F Real estate professionals never recommend one form of ownership over another. |
| 55. An easement by prescription is an example of voluntary alienation. | F involuntary alienation |
| 56. A survey is important in revealing a zoning violation or an encroachment that is not public record. | T |
| 57. If a developer wants to establish home sites on vacant land that is within the city, he should subdivide the land by use of lot and block. | T |

| | | |
|---|---|---|
| 58. | A survey or improvement location certificate (ILC) would be used to locate setbacks and find encroachments. | T |
| 59. | A township contains 640 acres. | F A section contains 640 acres; a township contains 36 sections. |
| 60. | The multiple listing service files provide the *BEST* legal description of property. | F survey, deed, or title work |
| 61. | The *BEST* source of legal description is the land survey. | T |
| 62. | The legal description of a lot with a new house in a platted subdivision should include the block and lot number. | T |
| 63. | A metes-and-bounds description uses sections and townships as part of the description. | F feet and compass degrees |
| 64. | Many financial institutions require a survey on newly constructed property before making a loan. | T |
| 65. | The U.S. government survey method of description makes use of sections, meridians, and townships. | T |
| 66. | Monuments are used to locate historic sites. | F boundaries |
| 67. | The method of legal description that utilizes plat maps is metes and bounds. | F lot and block |
| 68. | A property description using monuments, degrees, feet, distances, and compass directions is metes and bounds. | T |
| 69. | A developer must record the plat before acquiring building permits. | T |
| 70. | Zoning is an example of private controls on land use. | F public control/police power |
| 71. | Deed restrictions are an example of public controls on land use. | F private control |
| 72. | Restrictive covenants apply only to subdivisions. | F may be added to any deed |
| 73. | An article that was once personal property but has been more or less permanently installed or attached to the land or a building is known as personal property. | F fixture |
| 74. | A freestanding, custom-built bookcase would be considered personal property. | T key—freestanding |
| 75. | The interest in property held by a person who is granted lifetime use of a property that will be transferred to a third party upon the death of the lifetime user is a life estate. | T |
| 76. | The owner of Parcel 1 has the benefit of a right-of-way easement across Parcel 2. The owner of Parcel 1 is referred to as the servient estate. | F dominant estate |
| 77. | An encumbrance is also known as an imperfection. | T |
| 78. | A deed states the property may never be used to sell alcohol. This is a deed condition. | T |
| 79. | A lessor holds a leasehold estate. | F leased fee estate |
| 80. | Flight paths, coastal preservation, floodplains, or any special use that impacts the property must be disclosed. | T |
| 81. | Any outstanding claim or encumbrance that impairs an owner's title to real estate is known as a cloud on title. | T |

| | | |
|---|---|---|
| **82.** | Land is considered a liquid asset. | F Because it can take time to sell, land is not considered liquid. |
| **83.** | Fixtures are attached to the land. | F to improvements |
| **84.** | Land is considered a fixture. | F Fixtures are attached to improvements, which are attached to land. |
| **85.** | The owner of a life estate in property pays the real estate taxes. | T |
| **86.** | An easement does *NOT* transfer with the sale of the land. | F transfers unless released by the holder |
| **87.** | Trade fixtures and emblements are personal property. | T |
| **88.** | A farmer purchased land with no access to a street or public way. The seller owns adjoining property with access. After an unsuccessful attempt to gain access through negotiation, if the farmer was able to gain access across the seller's property, it was probably through an easement by necessity. | T |
| **89.** | A grandmother owned a life estate measured by her own life in residence. She leased the property for 5 years using a standard lease contract. Shortly thereafter, she died. The lease was valid for up to 1 year after her death. | F valid only as long as she was alive |
| **90.** | An electrician did some rewiring in a home, for which she has not yet been paid. One month after the work was completed, the electrician drove by the home to discover a For Sale sign on the property. The electrician should seek a quiet title action. | F She should file a mechanic's lien. |
| **91.** | An acre of land has 43,560 square feet. | T |
| **92.** | A homeowner employed a contractor to build a swimming pool on his property. Upon completion of the swimming pool, the contractor filed a lien to receive payment of the contract fee. Such filing could be considered a general lien. | F mechanic's lien, which is a specific lien |
| **93.** | Mark and Matt own adjoining parcels of real estate. Mark has granted Matt an easement over his property for ingress and egress. If Matt decides to sell his land to Jim, the status of the dominant and servient estates would not change. | T |
| **94.** | A built-in bookcase would be transferred as part of the real estate using a deed. | T |
| **95.** | Tenancy in common allows two sisters to take title to income property in unequal shares. | T |
| **96.** | An individual's property is taken by the city and used for a new road. This is an example of eminent domain. | T |
| **97.** | Legal descriptions may be based on an informal street address. | F They may be based on the government survey, metes and bounds, or a subdivision plat. |
| **98.** | A land description that begins at a specific point and proceeds around the boundaries of a parcel by feet and compass degrees is an example of government survey. | F metes and bounds |
| **99.** | Base lines run east and west in a government survey. | T |
| **100.** | A section contains 160 acres. | F 640 acres |

101. A plumber sells his home, in which he has installed washerless faucets. After the contract has been executed, he decides to replace the faucets with standard faucets. The plumber can be held liable for removing the faucets because they are fixtures that were in place at the time the contract was signed.

T

102. A lien for unpaid special assessments is a general lien.

F specific lien

**QST   Which of the following would be considered to be fixtures?**

103. Refrigerator

F personal property

104. Electrical wiring

T

105. Trade fixtures

F personal property

106. Custom-built, freestanding entertainment center

F Freestanding makes it personal property.

107. Plumbing and heating fixtures

T

108. Emblements

F personal property

109. Section 21 is directly south of section 14 in a township.

F section 23 is south of 14

110. In order for personal property to be conveyed it must be listed in the MLS.

F the purchase agreement and bill of sale

111. Easements do NOT transfer with the deed.

F easements transfer

112. A property you list has a garage that extends onto the property of a neighbor. You should recommend that the seller obtain a permit for the garage.

F Note the encroachment on the listing agreement and recommend seller see attorney.

113. Fixtures are determined by the intent of the party attaching them.

T

114. Trade fixtures automatically transfer with the property.

F do not transfer because they are personal property

115. Plumbing and electrical wiring that is attached would automatically transfer with the property.

T They are fixtures.

116. Fixtures, rights, benefits, and any other appurtenances are conveyed with a bill of sale.

F deed

117. Leasehold estates are of an indefinite duration.

F They will, or can, be terminated.

118. Freehold estates have an indefinite duration.

T

119. A holder of a qualified fee estate could lose her property rights if she broke, or did not follow, deed condition.

T

120. Fee simple absolute can also be called a fee estate or fee simple estate.

T

121. The holder of a reversionary interest for a qualified fee estate might be able to obtain title if the condition is broken.

T

122. The owner of the property in a life estate is called the life tenant.

T

123. The holder of the remainder interest will have a fee simple estate upon the death of the life tenant.

T

124. The holders of the reversionary and remainder interest will both have a fee simple estate upon the death of the life tenant.

F There can only be a reversionary or remainder interest, not both. The holder will have fee simple.

| | |
|---|---|
| **125.** Upon the death of the life tenant, the holder of the reversionary interest will have a fee simple estate. | T |
| **126.** The holder of an estate/tenancy for years must give 30 days' notice prior to terminating the lease. | F no notice |
| **127.** A periodic tenancy renews upon payment of rent. | T |
| **128.** An estate for years continues until terminated by the owner or tenant. | F Must have a definite termination date |
| **129.** Easements are rights of possession. | F rights of use |
| **130.** An appurtenant easement has only a servient interest. | F two interests—dominant and servient |
| **131.** An easement by necessity would be given to the government or a utility company. | F only private owners |
| **132.** An easement along the rear of a property for cable TV is most likely an easement in gross. | T |
| **133.** Easements need to be in writing and are revocable. | F They must be in writing but are NOT revocable. |
| **134.** Licenses are non-revocable agreements. | F revocable |
| **135.** Easements transfer in the deed unless the holder of the easement releases the easement. | T |
| **136.** A seller buys an easement for a driveway from an adjacent owner at closing. The buyer will then have an easement, which is a fixture. | F appurtenance |
| **137.** For emblements, trade fixtures, and personal property to transfer with the property, the buyer must have the implied consent of the seller. | F expressed written consent |
| **138.** A legal description that uses direction and degrees is lot and block. | F metes and bounds |
| **139.** After obtaining a plat map, the developer's second step is to sell the lots. | F record the plat map |
| **140.** A private deed restriction that does not allow people of Swedish dissent to purchase property is legal. | F illegal |
| **141.** A developer could limit RV storage and require only wood fencing be used in the development by using deed restrictions. | T |
| **142.** The buyer must agree for an easement to transfer at closing. | F easements transfer with the land |
| **143.** Street addresses, as used in urban areas, are considered distinct enough to be used as legal descriptions for transferring real estate. | F street address can change |
| **144.** In a cooperative apartment house, the owner-occupants are share-holders of the corporation that owns the building. | T |
| **145.** The condominium form of ownership may be used for offices. | T Condominium can be any type of property. |
| **146.** An owner of a condominium or a cooperative might have to get permission from other owners to sell her unit or shares of stock. | T first right of refusal |
| **147.** A building owned by a corporation and subdivided into several portions, with each user owning stock in the corporation that owns the property, is a condominium. | F cooperative |
| **148.** A condominium can be industrial property. | T |

149. A unit in a condominium building and its common element interest are eligible for title insurance as a separate piece of property.

T

150. An owner of a condominium owns and can finance her unit.

T

151. The common elements are owned by all current owners as joint tenants.

F tenants in common

152. You have purchased the right to live in a condominium in a resort during the 32nd complete week of each calendar year. This type of ownership is MOST likely a town house.

F time-share

153. An owner of a condominium project does NOT have to pay mortgages, taxes, and assessments that are liens against other units in the project.

T

154. A difference between a cooperative and a condominium is that the condominium owner has shares of stocks, while the cooperative owner owns and finances his unit.

F Condo owner owns the unit; the cooperative owner owns shares of stock.

155. A condominium features fee simple ownership in the home and lot, plus an undivided interest in the common elements.

T

156. Owners of condominiums, cooperatives, and town houses all pay assessments or association fees.

T

157. Commercial property includes parking lots, office buildings, and shopping centers.

T

158. A property manager should try and attract high-quality tenants.

T

159. In order for the owner to build and operate commercial real estate, the property typically must be zoned for business purposes.

T

160. An office building, gas station, and parking lot are all examples of mixed property.

F commercial property

161. A business and its goodwill and assets are collectively referred to as a business opportunity.

T

162. In order to list and sell a business opportunity for another for a fee, one must hold a special business opportunity license.

F real estate broker's license

163. When transferring major inventory in bulk, as in the sale of a business, the seller must deliver an itemized list of property and identify creditors, if any.

T bulk transfer disclosure

164. The Uniform Commercial Code (UCC) requires bulk sales disclosures in the sale of goods valued at $500,000 or more.

F $500 or more

165. Ownership of stock in a corporation that owns a building is possibly a cooperative.

T

166. Time-shares are MOST common in resorts.

T

167. An owner of a time-share owns the property for a certain time each year.

T

168. Common interest properties often have rules and regulations on use, ownership, and changes to the property owners can make.

T

# LAND-USE CONTROLS AND REGULATIONS

(Test questions: Salesperson 5; Broker 5)

| | | |
|---|---|---|
| 1. | Police power is the public control of land use. | T |
| 2. | Zoning, building permits, and other safety issues are part of the government's right of escheat. | F police power |
| 3. | Property taxes are based on market value. | F assessed value |
| 4. | A homeowner can appeal a property tax assessment to the assessor's appeals board. | T |
| 5. | Property tax reassessments cannot be appealed. | F to the assessor's appeals board |
| 6. | Property tax reassessments can be appealed to a district court. | F to the assessor's appeals board |
| 7. | A developer requires that all houses in a new subdivision have attached garages. This is an example of a building code. | F deed restriction or covenant |
| 8. | A new residential development might have a covenant requiring no chain link fences and that only those of German descent can live in the development. | F may restrict fencing but cannot break fair housing laws |
| 9. | Zoning laws are determined by state and federal law. | F set at local, city, or county level |
| 10. | A requirement that all commercial buildings have at *LEAST* one bathroom for every 3,000 square feet is an example of a safety code. | F building code |
| 11. | A purchaser who wishes to use the property for something other than its zoned use should apply for a reassessment. | F variance or special exception |
| 12. | Land that separates two different land uses is called a buffer zone. | T |
| 13. | One of the powers of the state that may affect privately owned real property is known as defeasance. | F police power, taxation, eminent domain, escheat (PETE) |
| 14. | Even though unrecorded, a lien for property taxes and a lien for special assessments would have priority over a first mortgage. | T |
| 15. | The term *escheat* means the right of the government to take private property for public use. | F right is eminent domain |
| 16. | If a person has no heirs and leaves no will, her property will be disposed of by eminent domain. | F escheat |
| 17. | The government may acquire ownership of privately owned real estate by the process of condemnation. The right is called police power. | F eminent domain |
| 18. | A special assessment could be found by reviewing the assessment rolls. | T |
| 19. | Zoning, nuisance abatement, safety codes, and building codes are examples of land-use controls under the concept of police power. | T |
| 20. | Fair and just compensation must be paid to the owner of a property when the government exercises eminent domain. | T |
| 21. | Master development plans used by *MOST* cities would normally include an analysis of the recent and projected population growth within the geographic area served by the community. | T |
| 22. | A planned unit development (PUD) is a planned mix of diverse land uses in one overall comprehensive plan. | T |

| | | |
|---|---|---|
| 23. | An area is zoned for residential use. A retail store is already located within this area. The store is an example of a variance. | F nonconforming use |
| 24. | As used in connection with real estate, a variance is a court order prohibiting certain activities in an area. | F permission to vary to prevent economic hardship |
| 25. | Water rights based on first beneficial use are called riparian rights. | F doctrine of prior appropriation |
| 26. | A lot that is 50 feet by 100 feet would have a frontage of 100 feet. | F The frontage is the first number, so it is 50 feet. |
| 27. | A city may enforce its zoning laws by requiring a building permit before a structure is constructed. | T |
| 28. | The use of a property that was lawful at the time of enactment but is now in violation of a zoning regulation is an example of spot zoning. | F nonconforming use |
| 29. | Zoning regulations can limit the rights of property owners by controlling the use of the land. | T |
| 30. | Zoning regulations can limit the rights of property owners by limiting the density of the population on the land. | T |
| 31. | A zoning district has been approved for light industrial use. A property owner within the district is permitted to continue to use his property for commercial purposes. This results in a nonconforming use. | T |
| 32. | A daycare facility that is operating in a residential zoning MOST likely has nonconforming use. | F special or conditional use |
| 33. | An exception to a zoning regulation that permits a landowner to deviate from zoning requirements in cases where strict enforcement would impose undue hardship is known as an amendment. | F variance |
| 34. | A buyer wants to sell crafts from the residential property he is purchasing. This is allowed under residential zoning. | F Buyer should call zoning board to verify if the use is allowed. |
| 35. | A real estate professional is responsible for determining if the zoning is correct and applying for any variances or special-use permits for buyers. | F should advise buyer to contact zoning board to determine if use is allowed and what may be required |
| 36. | Zoning restrictions are created primarily to protect against uncontrolled growth. | T |
| 37. | Municipalities require submission of blueprints and construction plans prior to issuing a building permit to control the influx of builders from surrounding areas. | F to ensure compliance with building codes and regulations |
| 38. | An area of land that separates two drastically different land use zones is a nonconforming zone. | F buffer zone |
| 39. | When the county board acquires land for a freeway, it is exercising the power of eminent domain. | T |
| 40. | One example of the use of police power by a city is environmental protection laws. | T |
| 41. | An office building existed before the land was zoned residential by a new zoning ordinance. The office building is an example of a variance. | F nonconforming use |

| | | |
|---|---|---|
| 42. | A homeowner who wants to build a fence that is above the height limit set by zoning needs to get a special-use permit in order to build the fence. | F variance |
| 43. | Tax assessments can be appealed to the treasury. | F assessors appeal board |
| 44. | Property taxes and special assessments take priority over other liens. | T |
| 45. | Master plans are used to control growth. | T |
| 46. | Zoning laws determine what type of construction is allowed. | T |
| 47. | An owner who wanted to deviate from a building code would seek a special-use permit. | F variance |
| 48. | A new owner of a property with a conditional use permit will automatically have the same rights of use as the current owner. | F special or conditional use may not transfer to new owners |
| 49. | A certificate of occupancy confirms that the property meets building codes. | T |
| 50. | Building codes determine the type and use of materials, such as plumbing or electrical. | T |
| 51. | A property owner who wants to build into the setback will need to get a variance. | T |

QST  Police power controls include:

| | | |
|---|---|---|
| 52. | Zoning | T |
| 53. | Building codes | T |
| 54. | Deed restrictions | F private control |
| 55. | Promoting general welfare | T |
| 56. | Private land-use controls | F |
| | | |
| 57. | A tire company has a manufacturing plant located in an area that recently has been zoned residential. The company is allowed to operate under the new zoning ordinance. If the plant is destroyed by fire, the company is likely to get permission to reconstruct the tire plant. | F It is a legal nonconforming use, but the company is unlikely to get a building permit for rebuilding it. |
| 58. | Eminent domain provides for monetary compensation to an owner in the event of a loss of property value as a result of condemnation. | T |
| 59. | The doctrine of prior appropriation states that the first beneficial user of water will have senior rights. | T |
| 60. | An environmental impact statement is required for all past government projects. | F proposed or future |
| 61. | A retail store in a residential area is an example of nonconforming use. | T |

QST  Improvements that would result in a special assessment include:

| | | |
|---|---|---|
| 62. | Building an addition to your house | F |
| 63. | Improvements to the curb and gutter system | T |
| 64. | Commercial window replacement due to hail damage | F |

| | | |
|---|---|---|
| **65.** | The type of value that is MOST relevant in determining property taxes is the appraised value. | F assessed value |
| **66.** | An assessment of taxes on real property according to value is known as market value. | F ad valorem |
| **67.** | If an owner failed to pay his property taxes, the property will eventually be sold at a public tax sale auction, and the proceeds will be used to pay the delinquent taxes. | T |
| **68.** | Property taxation is an example of a private right. | F government right |
| **69.** | The mill rate can be determined by dividing the tax rate by 1,000. | T |
| **70.** | Tax levies on property owners to pay for street improvements are called special assessments. | T |
| **71.** | Special tax districts, school and overlay zoning, or airports are examples of exceptional or special-use zoning. | T |
| **72.** | A seller has knowledge of an environmental impact report that is being done on a nearby industrial park. Since the report is not complete, the seller does NOT have to disclose the report. | F Since the report may impact the value and the buyer's decision, this is a material fact that must be disclosed. |
| **73.** | A lien against property that benefits from public improvements is known as a general lien. | F specific lien for special assessments |
| **74.** | Area preference refers to people's choices and desires to live in a given area. | T |
| **75.** | Although there is a substantial amount of unused land, supply in a given location or of a specific quality can be limited. This economic characteristic of land is referred to as scarcity. | T |
| **76.** | A builder is planning a subdivision zoned residential. Through a covenant in the deed, he states, "No one can babysit or provide child care other than for their own children, on a daily or continual basis, for more than one child." This would be considered a public control on land use. | F private control |
| **77.** | Master plans are used to stop growth. | F control growth |
| **78.** | Special assessments take priority over other liens. | T |
| **79.** | All property taxes or special assessments owed are public records and therefore do NOT need to be disclosed. | F should be disclosed |
| **80.** | It is illegal for deed restrictions or covenants to restrict access based on race or national origin. | T |
| **81.** | Condemnation is part of the process of escheat. | F eminent domain |

# SPECIALTY AREAS

(Test questions: Salesperson 2; Broker 3)

1. The two forms of eviction are sheriff's and constructive. | F actual and constructive
2. A tenant who is renting a commercial property pays a certain percentage of the gross sales profit of the business in addition to the base rent. This is an example of a percentage lease. | T
3. A tenant who has rented a residential property for a long period of time agrees to pay a slightly higher rent each year of her lease. This is an example of a ground lease. | F graduated/step-up
4. A tenant who is renting a residential property is allowed to apply rental payments to the purchase of the property. This is an example of a sale-leaseback. | F rent with option to buy
5. A gross lease is one whereby the landlord pays all property charges and the tenant pays a fixed monthly rent. | T
6. A lease must be in writing to be enforceable, unless it is for a time period of one year or less. | T
7. A tenant who has cause to use constructive eviction may give the landlord notice that she is not paying rent but will stay in the property until the complaints are resolved. | F Tenants using constructive eviction must move out.
8. In accounting for expenditures made on behalf of the principal, a manager of an apartment complex should consider maintenance, personnel salaries, and real estate taxes as operating expenses. | T
9. A landlord gave a tenant a two-year lease. The landlord died at the end of the first year, and the property was sold. The tenant must vacate the property. | F The tenant's rights are not terminated by the death or sale and continue until the end of the lease term.
10. Under conditions of climbing inflation, a property manager would be reluctant to negotiate a fixed lease. | T
11. A lease where the tenant pays a percentage of the monthly building expenses is a percentage lease. | F net lease
12. A commercial tenant that pays only rent has a fixed or gross lease. | T
13. A buyer of a commercial property that is currently leased would normally be entitled to take immediate possession. | F Buyers take title subject to, and must honor, the existing lease.
14. If a developer leases real property from the owner with the intent of constructing an office building on it, the developer holds a leasehold interest. | T

# MANDATED DISCLOSURES

(Test questions: Salesperson 8; Broker 9)

| | | |
|---|---|---|
| 1. | A salesperson informed by the seller that there is a problem with a leaky roof must inform a prospective buyer of these conditions. | T |
| 2. | A seller of a property that was built in 1988 will need to give the buyer a lead-based paint disclosure. | F  only prior to January 1, 1978 |

**QST Lead could be found in the following:**

| | | |
|---|---|---|
| 3. | Paint | T |
| 4. | Insulation | F |
| 5. | Flooring | F |
| 6. | House paint after 1978 | F |
| 7. | Pipes | T |
| 8. | Soil | T |
| 9. | A seller who is selling "as is" does not have to disclose any material facts. | F  Must disclose; "as is" means seller won't make repairs. |
| 10. | Radon, mold, and asbestos may require mitigation, cleanup, or abatement. | T |
| 11. | A seller tells the broker the radon issue has been solved, but the broker suspects it may still be an issue. The broker does *NOT* have to disclose because the broker's duty is to the seller. | F  Real estate professionals must disclose all material facts or suspicions if they believe they might change a buyer's decision. |
| 12. | Radon and carbon monoxide are colorless and odorless gases that can cause harm or death. | T |
| 13. | Asbestos encapsulation is often a safer and better solution than abatement or removal. | T |
| 14. | All mold is considered toxic and must be removed. | F  Many molds are beneficial. |
| 15. | Lead-based paint disclosures allow the buyer to waive the right to an inspection. | T |
| 16. | Sellers must remove all known lead-based paint. | F  must disclose, not remove |
| 17. | Landlords must give tenants a lead-based paint disclosure if the property being rented was built before January 1, 1978 (memory aid: 1-1-78). | T |
| 18. | Environmental issues, known and latent material facts, and issues in the surrounding areas that might impact value are examples of stigmatized issues that do not have to be disclosed. | F  These are material facts that must be disclosed. |
| 19. | The EPA regulates *MOST* environmental issues, including lead-based paint. | T |
| 20. | Septic systems, back lines, and sealed wells should be mitigated. | F  disclosed |
| 21. | Environmental issues rarely impact value. | F  often impact value |

22. If a buyer's broker notices water marks in the basement, the broker should wait to ask the listing broker about the issue before disclosing to the buyer.

F immediately disclose to the buyer

23. Radon, mold, asbestos, lead-based paint, and other environmental hazards must be disclosed if they are known.

T

24. Radon is relatively easy to detect and inexpensive to mitigate.

T

# TRANSFER OF TITLE

(Test questions: Salesperson 5; Broker 5)

| | | |
|---|---|---|
| 1. | A title report would show all prior recorded encumbrances on a property. | F current encumbrances |
| 2. | A title report would show all prior owners of a property. | F An abstract or chain of title would show this; title report only shows current status. |
| 3. | An easement appurtenant is transferred by a deed. | T |
| 4. | A woman dies testate and leaves a property to her son in her will. The process used to transfer the property is escheat. | F The will goes through probate. |
| 5. | For personal or real property to transfer in a will, the will must go through probate. | T |
| 6. | If a deed is NOT recorded, later claims on title could potentially take priority. | T |
| 7. | Recording prevents later claims on title from taking priority over an unrecorded interest. | T |
| 8. | A deed of trust is the BEST deed for a purchaser to use to take title. | F General warranty deed, as a deed of trust, is used to create liens, not pass title. |
| 9. | The deed with the MOST warranties, providing the greatest protection for the buyer, is a general warranty deed. | T |
| 10. | An unrecorded deed lacks actual notice. | F constructive notice |
| 11. | Legal or constructive notice is created by recording documents. | T |
| 12. | Title insurance premiums are paid annually. | F once at closing |
| 13. | Title insurance differs from other types of insurance because the premium is paid only once at the beginning of the policy. | T |
| 14. | An estate for years is terminated when a property is sold. | F Sale of the property does not affect a leasehold estate. |
| 15. | Upon the sale of a property, the leasehold estate would automatically terminate unless it is renewed within 60 days of the sale. | F Leasehold estates survive the sale of a property. |
| 16. | A grantor can impose restrictions on the use of property in a deed. | T |
| 17. | The covenant of seisin states that the owner will defend the title. | F Seisin states the grantor has the right to convey. |
| 18. | A quitclaim deed would be used to limit claims or liability in the future. | T |
| 19. | A homeowner who has a warranty deed but still owes on her mortgage holds title to the land. | T |
| 20. | Upon the death of a joint tenancy owner, the property is probated and passed on to the owner's heirs or devisees. | F Joint tenancy does not go through probate, and title transfers directly to the other joint tenants. |
| 21. | A quitclaim deed could transfer clear title from the grantor without any guarantees against a cloud. | T |

| | |
|---|---|
| 22. Mr. Booth, a distant relative of a deceased property owner, may have a claim against the property. The attorney from the estate might ask Mr. Booth to execute an executor's deed. | F quitclaim deed |
| 23. The only form of conveyance in which the grantor specifically disclaims both warranties of title and ownership is a quitclaim deed. | T |
| 24. Mr. Barnes inherits a family farm that he has never seen and wants to sell it. He would be *BEST* protected from liability by using a general warranty deed. | F quitclaim or special warranty deed |
| 25. A quitclaim deed conveys the interest of the grantee. | F grantor |
| QST To be valid, a deed must: | |
| 26. Be recorded | F Recording gives constructive notice. |
| 27. Have words of conveyance | T |
| 28. Be signed by the grantor | T |
| 29. Be signed by the grantee | F grantor only |
| 30. Be delivered and accepted | T |
| 31. The primary purpose of a deed is to prove ownership and create a recordable record. | F transfer title |
| 32. A deed by which the grantor pledges to defend title forever against all claims is a warranty deed. | T |
| 33. To convey an entire property, a deed must contain an accurate description of the house and other improvements. | F Legal description of the land only needed; all other items are appurtenant. |
| 34. A will may be used to transfer property. | T |
| 35. A properly drawn and executed deed is considered to be legally delivered from the seller to the buyer when the deed is in the possession of the grantor. | F grantee |
| 36. The grantee's signature is among the essential elements of a valid deed. | F grantor signs |
| 37. A special warranty deed creates the greatest potential risk for the grantor. | F general warranty deed |
| 38. To convey ownership of a parcel of real estate, the grantor in the deed must be the owner shown by a current opinion of title or title examination. | T |
| 39. A summary of the recorded documents pertaining to the title to a property is a title commitment. | F abstract |
| 40. Consideration is among the essential elements of a valid deed. | T |
| 41. Constructive notice of a real estate sale is achieved by recording documents in the public records. | T |
| 42. Recording determines priority of loans. | T |
| 43. The warranty in a special warranty deed is against encumbrances created during the ownership of the grantor. | T |

| | | |
|---|---|---|
| **44.** | The gift of real property by will is known as a devise. | T |
| **45.** | Quiet enjoyment means that neighbors cannot disturb the owner with loud parties. | F The grantee will not be disturbed by claims of others. |
| **46.** | Recordation is essential to the validity of a deed. | F Title transfers upon delivery and acceptance. |
| **47.** | The best deed to limit liability and future claims is a special warranty deed. | F quitclaim |
| **48.** | Sorenson inherits a family ranch and discovers that the title is clouded. A quiet title suit may be needed to clear the title. | T |
| **49.** | The public recording system cures all title defects. | F allows the posting and searching of claims |
| **50.** | Documents should be acknowledged or notarized to show they were signed without duress. | T |
| **51.** | A gift of real property by will is a bequest. | F devise; bequest for personal property |
| **52.** | The deed that limits the grantor's warranty to the grantor's period of ownership is the general warranty deed. | F special warranty deed |
| **53.** | Regardless of the form of ownership, all owners need to sign the deed to convey full ownership to the new grantee. | T |
| **54.** | If an owner in severalty dies testate, the deceased's interests will be probated and passed to the deceased's heirs or devisees. | T |
| **55.** | Title searches and attorney's opinions are used to guarantee the buyer marketable title. | F There is no guarantee, or proof, of marketable title. |
| **56.** | When Adams recorded the deed he received, the legal consequence of recording was to serve constructive notice of Adams's ownership interest. | T |
| **57.** | For buyers, the *BEST* form of protection against loss of title would come in the form of an owner's title insurance policy. | T |
| **58.** | Title insurance covers defects and exceptions found prior to closing. | F defects found after closing |
| **59.** | A second mortgage can be distinguished from a first mortgage by the date it was recorded. | T |
| **60.** | The mortgagee's title insurance policy protects the borrower. | F lender |
| **61.** | The act of recording a deed is primarily of benefit to the grantee. | T |
| **62.** | A purchase agreement is usually recorded. | F Easements, deeds, long-term leases, and mortgages are recorded. |
| **63.** | Policies and procedures that regulate the recordation of documents for conveying rights and/or interests in real estate are established by federal law. | F state law |
| **64.** | The primary purpose of recording deeds and other legal documents is to provide constructive notice. | T |
| **65.** | A title search will reveal an encroachment. | F recorded encumbrances |
| **66.** | Actual notice is created by recording. | F by actual visual inspection of the property |

| | | |
|---|---|---|
| 67. | A cloud on title is MOST likely to be discovered in an appraisal report. | F title report or title opinion |
| 68. | A standard policy of title insurance would cover the problems created by a forged deed. | T |
| 69. | A deed must be acknowledged to be valid. | F should be acknowledged to be recorded |
| 70. | In a real estate transaction, a licensee should advise the buyer of the need for a title search. | T |
| 71. | Possession of real property passes at the time of delivery and acceptance of the deed, unless otherwise agreed. | T |
| 72. | The laws of the state in which a property is located govern the acquisition, transfer, and recordation of title to land. | T |
| 73. | An abstract of title contains all the actual documents from the chain of title. | F It contains a summary of the documents. |
| 74. | The government transfers real property to a private individual using a private grant. | F land patent |
| 75. | The covenant of seisin and covenant against encumbrances would be found in a quitclaim deed. | F general warranty deed |
| 76. | A prescriptive easement is gained through adverse use. | T |
| 77. | For a deed to be valid, it must contain the signature of the grantee. | F Grantors must sign. |
| 78. | The legal owner is unknown. The neighbor has no official deed to the land but was awarded title since he had lived on the property more than 18 years. This is an example of adverse possession. | T |
| 79. | Tenant A has been awarded an easement by necessity to cross Tenant B's property. This easement will terminate automatically after 15 years. | F Easements terminate only through merger, release, or abandonment. |
| 80. | A quitclaim deed can be used to terminate deed restrictions. | T |
| 81. | A bill of sale is used to convey title to real property. | F personal property |
| 82. | The cost of a title insurance policy that protects against defects in the title is paid once every year. | F once, when issued |
| 83. | A title insurance policy would include a summary of the links in the chain of title. | F would only include the current status |
| 84. | A deed must be executed by at LEAST two competent witnesses in order to be valid. | F must contain essential elements; no witnesses needed |
| 85. | Sale and transfer by deed is an example of voluntary alienation. | T |
| 86. | The government conveys title to property using a deed. | F land patent |
| 87. | An individual takes possession of an owner's land after obtaining the owner's permission. The possession continues for 26 years. Thereafter, the occupant attempts to get title to the property. The possessor will be unsuccessful because NOT all of the requirements for adverse possession have been satisfied. | T cannot have adverse possession with the owner's permission |
| 88. | Generally, title insurance coverage extends to exceptions listed in the policy. | F Only defects are NOT listed in the policy; exceptions are never covered. |

| | |
|---|---|
| 89. An individual seller who realizes a net profit of more than $250,000 from the sale of her personal residence may be required to pay a sales tax. | F capital gains tax |
| 90. A title commitment is a commitment to insure title. | T |
| 91. The mortgagee's policy protects the owner. | F lender |
| 92. The title policy is issued before the closing with the title commitment. | F at or after closing |
| 93. A property has a first mortgage for $100,000, and the property taxes of $4,500 have NOT been paid. The property tax lien will be in first position. | T |
| 94. A loan for $75,000 is recorded, after which a loan for $150,000 is recorded. The larger lien has priority. | F Priority is determined by when the lien was recorded. |
| 95. At the closing of a real estate transaction, continuing charges such as taxes and insurance premiums are prorated. | T |
| 96. Upon receiving an offer, the earnest money is deposited in a trust account. | F Only upon acceptance of the offer will the money be deposited. |
| 97. In order for the public to have constructive notice of a deed, it must be registered in the office of property. | F county recorder |
| 98. The grantee, under a recorded deed, can enforce the deed against the grantor. | T |
| 99. If a broker places earnest monies in his personal account, commingling has occurred. | T |
| 100. At closing, the purchase price is normally a credit to the buyer. | F Credit seller; debit buyer. |
| 101. The buyer's earnest money is normally a debit to the buyer. | F credit to buyer |
| 102. In a closing, the buyer normally pays for recording of a new mortgage. | T |
| 103. The sales commission will normally appear on the buyer's closing statement. | F seller's closing statement |
| 104. A loan origination fee would appear on the buyer's closing statement. | T |
| 105. At closing, the selling price is a credit to the seller. | T |
| 106. A new loan will be a credit to the buyer. | T Remember: Loans are always a buyer credit. |
| 107. A title search guarantees the buyer of marketable title. | F no guarantees |
| 108. A title search should disclose real estate tax liens, prior recorded mortgages, and unpaid judgments against the seller. | T |
| 109. The seller normally delivers the deed to the buyer when the sales contract is signed. | F at closing/settlement |
| 110. An up-to-date title abstract requires an attorney's opinion to explain the kind of title and its condition. | T |
| 111. In order for a buyer to make certain that a property she is purchasing has no encroachments, she should obtain a title search. | F survey or ILC |
| 112. A cloud on the title of a property would probably be revealed by the appraisal. | F title search |

113. The primary purpose of a closing statement is to provide a detailed accounting of the amount each party will receive or be required to pay at closing. | T

114. A buyer's earnest money will appear on the settlement statement as a credit to the seller and a credit to the buyer. | F credit buyer only

115. To determine the amount of cash the buyer will need at closing, the closing agent will subtract the buyer's total credits from the buyer's total debits. | T

116. The charge for a notary fee for the warranty deed will be a debit to the buyer. | F debit to the seller who signed it

**QST  Which items are deductible on income taxes?**

117. Points and origination fees | T

118. Property insurance | F

119. Principal | F

120. Mortgage interest | T

121. HOA dues | F

122. Property taxes | T  Remember POIT

123. Assumed loans are a credit to the buyer and a debit to the seller. | T  Remember: All loans are always a buyer credit.

124. Recording of the warranty deed is a debit to the seller. | F  Buyer records the deed.

125. Mortgagee's title policy will be a debit to the seller. | F  buyer

126. Rents are prorated between the buyer and the seller. | T

127. Security deposits are prorated between the buyer and the seller. | F  transferred in full to the buyer

128. A lender wanting title insurance coverage on property pledged as collateral would ask for an errors and omissions policy. | F  mortgagee's policy

129. A good-faith estimate is due at closing, and the HUD-1 is due upon application for a loan. | F  HUD-1 is due at closing; good-faith estimate is due at application.

130. An owner's policy for title insurance protects the owner and the lender. | F  owner and heirs while they have an interest

131. The government transfers government-owned real property to a private individual using a land patent. | T

132. The covenant of seisin and covenant against encumbrances would be found in a quitclaim deed. | F  general warranty deed

133. Investors often use accrued interest to depreciate property. | F straight line

134. A 1031 tax-deferred exchange is used by investors to defer capital gains taxes. | T

135. Variable and passive are two forms of depreciation used by investors. | F straight line

136. Investors are allowed to depreciate commercial property over 39 years. | T

137. A title commitment has the MOST historical information. | F  abstract

**138.** Joe has been walking across Sarah's property. Because both of them are aware of the use and Sarah gave Joe permission, Joe has a prescriptive easement.

F license

**139.** Loan origination fees are typically a debit to the seller.

F debit the buyer

**140.** Joe and Sally are selling their primary residence. They would benefit from using a 1031 exchange.

F 1031 exchanges are for investment property.

**141.** To receive a capital gains tax exclusion for a primary residence, the owner must live in the property for at *LEAST* 5 years.

F 2 out of 5 years

Self-Score Answer Sheets

National Test Prep Exam Prep 4E Self Score Answer Sheet   Broker

**Online students:** While you take the exam online, also mark your answers on this sheet. After completing the exam, mark which answers you did not get correct on this sheet.

**All students:** Write the correct answer next to those questions you answered incorrectly. Add up your scores for each category and then add up your overall score. Be sure to have this answer sheet with you during the course.

**Student Name:** _____

**Test (circle one):** _____ Pre-Test / Post-Test

### Valuation and Market Analysis
(6 questions)

1. _____
2. _____
3. _____
4. _____
5. _____
6. _____

Total correct: _____

### Financing
(7 questions)

7. _____
8. _____
9. _____
10. _____
11. _____
12. _____
13. _____

Total correct: _____

### Contracts
(12 questions)

14. _____
15. _____
16. _____
17. _____
18. _____
19. _____
20. _____
21. _____
22. _____
23. _____
24. _____
25. _____

Total correct: _____

### Math
(4 questions)

26. _____
27. _____
28. _____
29. _____

Total correct: _____

### Property Ownership (30–35)
(6 questions);
### Transfer of Title (36–40)
(5 questions)

30. _____
31. _____
32. _____
33. _____
34. _____
35. _____

Total correct: _____

36. _____
37. _____
38. _____
39. _____
40. _____

Total correct: _____

### Land Use Controls and Regulations
(5 questions)

41. _____
42. _____
43. _____
44. _____
45. _____

Total correct: _____

### General Principles of Agency
(11 questions)

46. _____
47. _____
48. _____
49. _____
50. _____
51. _____
52. _____
53. _____
54. _____
55. _____
56. _____

Total correct: _____

### Mandated Disclosures
(9 questions)

57. _____
58. _____
59. _____
60. _____
61. _____
62. _____
63. _____
64. _____
65. _____

Total correct: _____

### Practice of Real Estate
(12 questions)

66. _____
67. _____
68. _____
69. _____
70. _____
71. _____
72. _____
73. _____
74. _____
75. _____
76. _____
77. _____

Total correct: _____

### Specialty Areas
(3 questions)

78. _____
79. _____
80. _____

Total correct: _____

©2014 Kaplan, Inc. Published by DF Institute, Inc., d/b/a Kaplan Real Estate Education. Printed in the United States of America. All rights reserved. The text of this publication, or any part thereof, may not be reproduced in any manner whatsoever without written permission from the publisher.
ISBN: 0-X214-3520-4   PPN: 2143-5204

National PSI Exam Prep 4L Self-Score Answer Sheet – Broker

**Online students:** While you take the exam online, also mark your answers on this sheet. After completing the exam, mark which answers you did not get correct on this sheet.

**All students:** Write the correct answer next to those questions you answered incorrectly. Add up your scores for each category and then add up your overall score. Be sure to have this answer sheet with you during the course.

**Student Name:** _____

**Test (circle one):** _____ Pre-Test / Post-Test

| Valuation and Market Analysis (6 questions) | Financing (7 questions) | Contracts (12 questions) | Math (4 questions) | Property Ownership (30–35) (6 questions); Transfer of Title (36–40) (5 questions) |
|---|---|---|---|---|
| 1. ___ | 7. ___ | 14. ___ | 26. ___ | 30. ___ |
| 2. ___ | 8. ___ | 15. ___ | 27. ___ | 31. ___ |
| 3. ___ | 9. ___ | 16. ___ | 28. ___ | 32. ___ |
| 4. ___ | 10. ___ | 17. ___ | 29. ___ | 33. ___ |
| 5. ___ | 11. ___ | 18. ___ | Total correct: ___ | 34. ___ |
| 6. ___ | 12. ___ | 19. ___ | | 35. ___ |
| Total correct: ___ | 13. ___ | 20. ___ | | Total correct: ___ |
| | Total correct: ___ | 21. ___ | | 36. ___ |
| | | 22. ___ | | 37. ___ |
| | | 23. ___ | | 38. ___ |
| | | 24. ___ | | 39. ___ |
| | | 25. ___ | | 40. ___ |
| | | Total correct: ___ | | Total correct: ___ |

| Land Use Controls and Regulations (5 questions) | General Principles of Agency (11 questions) | Mandated Disclosures (9 questions) | Practice of Real Estate (12 questions) | Specialty Areas (3 questions) |
|---|---|---|---|---|
| 41. ___ | 46. ___ | 57. ___ | 66. ___ | 78. ___ |
| 42. ___ | 47. ___ | 58. ___ | 67. ___ | 79. ___ |
| 43. ___ | 48. ___ | 59. ___ | 68. ___ | 80. ___ |
| 44. ___ | 49. ___ | 60. ___ | 69. ___ | Total correct: ___ |
| 45. ___ | 50. ___ | 61. ___ | 70. ___ | |
| Total correct: ___ | 51. ___ | 62. ___ | 71. ___ | |
| | 52. ___ | 63. ___ | 72. ___ | |
| | 53. ___ | 64. ___ | 73. ___ | |
| | 54. ___ | 65. ___ | 74. ___ | |
| | 55. ___ | Total correct: ___ | 75. ___ | |
| | 56. ___ | | 76. ___ | |
| | Total correct: ___ | | 77. ___ | |
| | | | Total correct: ___ | |

©2014 Kaplan, Inc. Published by DF Institute, Inc., d/b/a Kaplan Real Estate Education. Printed in the United States of America. All rights reserved. The text of this publication, or any part thereof, may not be reproduced in any manner whatsoever without written permission from the publisher. ISBN: 0-X214-3520-4    PPN: 2143-5204

National Exam Prep 4L Self-Score Answer Sheet – Broker

**Online students:** While you take the exam online, also mark your answers on this sheet. After completing the exam, mark which answers you did not get correct on this sheet.

**All students:** Write the correct answer next to those questions you answered incorrectly. Add up your scores for each category and then add up your overall score. Be sure to have this answer sheet with you during the course.

**Student Name:** _____

**Test (circle one):** _____ Pre-Test / Post-Test

## Valuation and Market Analysis (6 questions)

1. ___
2. ___
3. ___
4. ___
5. ___
6. ___

Total correct: ___

## Financing (7 questions)

7. ___
8. ___
9. ___
10. ___
11. ___
12. ___
13. ___

Total correct: ___

## Contracts (12 questions)

14. ___
15. ___
16. ___
17. ___
18. ___
19. ___
20. ___
21. ___
22. ___
23. ___
24. ___
25. ___

Total correct: ___

## Math (4 questions)

26. ___
27. ___
28. ___
29. ___

Total correct: ___

## Property Ownership (30–35) (6 questions); Transfer of Title (36–40) (5 questions)

30. ___
31. ___
32. ___
33. ___
34. ___
35. ___

Total correct: ___

36. ___
37. ___
38. ___
39. ___
40. ___

Total correct: ___

## Land Use Controls and Regulations (5 questions)

41. ___
42. ___
43. ___
44. ___
45. ___

Total correct: ___

## General Principles of Agency (11 questions)

46. ___
47. ___
48. ___
49. ___
50. ___
51. ___
52. ___
53. ___
54. ___
55. ___
56. ___

Total correct: ___

## Mandated Disclosures (9 questions)

57. ___
58. ___
59. ___
60. ___
61. ___
62. ___
63. ___
64. ___
65. ___

Total correct: ___

## Practice of Real Estate (12 questions)

66. ___
67. ___
68. ___
69. ___
70. ___
71. ___
72. ___
73. ___
74. ___
75. ___
76. ___
77. ___

Total correct: ___

## Specialty Areas (3 questions)

78. ___
79. ___
80. ___

Total correct: ___

National PSI Exam Prep Pre-Test Score Answer Sheet — Salesperson

**Online students:** While you take the exam online, also mark your answers on this sheet. After completing the exam, mark which answers you did not get correct on this sheet.

**All students:** Write the correct answer next to those questions you answered incorrectly. Add up your scores for each category and then add up your overall score. Be sure to have this answer sheet with you during the course.

**Student Name:** _____

**Test (circle one):** _____ Pre-Test / Post-Test

| Valuation and Market Analysis (8 questions) | Financing (6 questions) | Contracts (11 questions) | Math (6 questions) | Property Ownership (32–38) (7 questions); Transfer of Title (39–43) (5 questions) |
|---|---|---|---|---|
| 1. _____ | 9. _____ | 15. _____ | 26. _____ | 32. _____ |
| 2. _____ | 10. _____ | 16. _____ | 27. _____ | 33. _____ |
| 3. _____ | 11. _____ | 17. _____ | 28. _____ | 34. _____ |
| 4. _____ | 12. _____ | 18. _____ | 29. _____ | 35. _____ |
| 5. _____ | 13. _____ | 19. _____ | 30. _____ | 36. _____ |
| 6. _____ | 14. _____ | 20. _____ | 31. _____ | 37. _____ |
| 7. _____ | Total correct: _____ | 21. _____ | Total correct: _____ | 38. _____ |
| 8. _____ | | 22. _____ | | Total correct: _____ |
| Total correct: _____ | | 23. _____ | | 39. _____ |
| | | 24. _____ | | 40. _____ |
| | | 25. _____ | | 41. _____ |
| | | Total correct: _____ | | 42. _____ |
| | | | | 43. _____ |
| | | | | Total correct: _____ |

| Land Use Controls and Regulations (5 questions) | General Principles of Agency (10 questions) | Mandated Disclosures (8 questions) | Practice of Real Estate (12 questions) | Specialty Areas (2 questions) |
|---|---|---|---|---|
| 44. _____ | 49. _____ | 59. _____ | 67. _____ | 79. _____ |
| 45. _____ | 50. _____ | 60. _____ | 68. _____ | 80. _____ |
| 46. _____ | 51. _____ | 61. _____ | 69. _____ | Total correct: _____ |
| 47. _____ | 52. _____ | 62. _____ | 70. _____ | |
| 48. _____ | 53. _____ | 63. _____ | 71. _____ | |
| Total correct: _____ | 54. _____ | 64. _____ | 72. _____ | |
| | 55. _____ | 65. _____ | 73. _____ | |
| | 56. _____ | 66. _____ | 74. _____ | |
| | 57. _____ | Total correct: _____ | 75. _____ | |
| | 58. _____ | | 76. _____ | |
| | Total correct: _____ | | 77. _____ | |
| | | | 78. _____ | |
| | | | Total correct: _____ | |

**Online students:** While you take the exam online, also mark your answers on this sheet. After completing the exam, mark which answers you did not get correct on this sheet.

**All students:** Write the correct answer next to those questions you answered incorrectly. Add up your scores for each category and then add up your overall score. Be sure to have this answer sheet with you during the course.

**Student Name:** _____

**Test (circle one):** _____ Pre-Test / Post-Test

| Valuation and Market Analysis (8 questions) | Financing (6 questions) | Contracts (11 questions) | Math (6 questions) | Property Ownership (32–38) (7 questions); Transfer of Title (39–43) (5 questions) |
|---|---|---|---|---|
| 1. _____ | 9. _____ | 15. _____ | 26. _____ | 32. _____ |
| 2. _____ | 10. _____ | 16. _____ | 27. _____ | 33. _____ |
| 3. _____ | 11. _____ | 17. _____ | 28. _____ | 34. _____ |
| 4. _____ | 12. _____ | 18. _____ | 29. _____ | 35. _____ |
| 5. _____ | 13. _____ | 19. _____ | 30. _____ | 36. _____ |
| 6. _____ | 14. _____ | 20. _____ | 31. _____ | 37. _____ |
| 7. _____ | Total correct: ____ | 21. _____ | Total correct: ____ | 38. _____ |
| 8. _____ | | 22. _____ | | Total correct: ____ |
| Total correct: ____ | | 23. _____ | | 39. _____ |
| | | 24. _____ | | 40. _____ |
| | | 25. _____ | | 41. _____ |
| | | Total correct: ____ | | 42. _____ |
| | | | | 43. _____ |
| | | | | Total correct: ____ |

| Land Use Controls and Regulations (5 questions) | General Principles of Agency (10 questions) | Mandated Disclosures (8 questions) | Practice of Real Estate (12 questions) | Specialty Areas (2 questions) |
|---|---|---|---|---|
| 44. _____ | 49. _____ | 59. _____ | 67. _____ | 79. _____ |
| 45. _____ | 50. _____ | 60. _____ | 68. _____ | 80. _____ |
| 46. _____ | 51. _____ | 61. _____ | 69. _____ | Total correct: ____ |
| 47. _____ | 52. _____ | 62. _____ | 70. _____ | |
| 48. _____ | 53. _____ | 63. _____ | 71. _____ | |
| Total correct: ____ | 54. _____ | 64. _____ | 72. _____ | |
| | 55. _____ | 65. _____ | 73. _____ | |
| | 56. _____ | 66. _____ | 74. _____ | |
| | 57. _____ | Total correct: ____ | 75. _____ | |
| | 58. _____ | | 76. _____ | |
| | Total correct: ____ | | 77. _____ | |
| | | | 78. _____ | |
| | | | Total correct: ____ | |

ISBN: 0-X214-3610-3    PPN: 2143-6103

**Online students:** While you take the exam online, also mark your answers on this sheet. After completing the exam, mark which answers you did not get correct on this sheet.

**All students:** Write the correct answer next to those questions you answered incorrectly. Add up your scores for each category and then add up your overall score. Be sure to have this answer sheet with you during the course.

**Student Name:** _____

**Test (circle one):** _____ Pre-Test / Post-Test

| Valuation and Market Analysis (8 questions) | Financing (6 questions) | Contracts (11 questions) | Math (6 questions) | Property Ownership (32–38) (7 questions); Transfer of Title (39–43) (5 questions) |
|---|---|---|---|---|
| 1. _____ | 9. _____ | 15. _____ | 26. _____ | 32. _____ |
| 2. _____ | 10. _____ | 16. _____ | 27. _____ | 33. _____ |
| 3. _____ | 11. _____ | 17. _____ | 28. _____ | 34. _____ |
| 4. _____ | 12. _____ | 18. _____ | 29. _____ | 35. _____ |
| 5. _____ | 13. _____ | 19. _____ | 30. _____ | 36. _____ |
| 6. _____ | 14. _____ | 20. _____ | 31. _____ | 37. _____ |
| 7. _____ | Total correct: _____ | 21. _____ | Total correct: _____ | 38. _____ |
| 8. _____ | | 22. _____ | | Total correct: _____ |
| Total correct: _____ | | 23. _____ | | 39. _____ |
| | | 24. _____ | | 40. _____ |
| | | 25. _____ | | 41. _____ |
| | | Total correct: _____ | | 42. _____ |
| | | | | 43. _____ |
| | | | | Total correct: _____ |

| Land Use Controls and Regulations (5 questions) | General Principles of Agency (10 questions) | Mandated Disclosures (8 questions) | Practice of Real Estate (12 questions) | Specialty Areas (2 questions) |
|---|---|---|---|---|
| 44. _____ | 49. _____ | 59. _____ | 67. _____ | 79. _____ |
| 45. _____ | 50. _____ | 60. _____ | 68. _____ | 80. _____ |
| 46. _____ | 51. _____ | 61. _____ | 69. _____ | Total correct: _____ |
| 47. _____ | 52. _____ | 62. _____ | 70. _____ | |
| 48. _____ | 53. _____ | 63. _____ | 71. _____ | |
| Total correct: _____ | 54. _____ | 64. _____ | 72. _____ | |
| | 55. _____ | 65. _____ | 73. _____ | |
| | 56. _____ | 66. _____ | 74. _____ | |
| | 57. _____ | Total correct: _____ | 75. _____ | |
| | 58. _____ | | 76. _____ | |
| | Total correct: _____ | | 77. _____ | |
| | | | 78. _____ | |
| | | | Total correct: _____ | |